IN DEFENSE
OF
POLITICAL TRIALS

IN DEFENSE
OF
POLITICAL TRIALS

Charles F. Abel & Frank H. Marsh

CONTRIBUTIONS IN POLITICAL SCIENCE, NUMBER 336
Bernard K. Johnpoll, *Series Editor*

Greenwood Press
WESTPORT, CONNECTICUT • LONDON

Library of Congress Cataloging-in-Publication Data

Abel, Charles F.
  In defense of political trials / Charles F. Abel and Frank H.
  Marsh.
        p.   cm.—(Contributions in political science, ISSN 0147–1066
  ; no. 336)
    Includes bibliographical references and index.
    ISBN 0–313–25111–8 (alk. paper)
    1. Courts—United States.   2. Political questions and judicial
  power—United States.   3. Law and politics.   I. Marsh, Frank H.
  II. Title.   III. Series.
  KF8700.A93   1994
  347.73′1—dc20
  [347.3071]   93–14129

British Library Cataloguing in Publication Data is available.

Library of Congress Catalog Card Number: 93–14129
ISBN: 0–313–25111–8
ISSN: 0147–1066

First published in 1994

Greenwood Press, 88 Post Road West, Westport, CT 06881
An imprint of Greenwood Publishing Group, Inc.

Printed in the United States of America

The paper used in this book complies with the
Permanent Paper Standard issued by the National
Information Standards Organization (Z39.48–1984).

10 9 8 7 6 5 4 3 2 1

Contents

Preface

We suspect that when most people think of a political trial they envision a man or woman standing before an array of black robed judges, defending themselves against the state's charges of treason, insurrection, heresy, or some peculiar crime that only exists in Eastern Europe or Asia, such as criticizing the prime minister or counterrevolutionary activities. Memorable trials of historical persons such as Socrates, Thomas More, or, more recently, Dietrich Bonhoffer are usually offered as definitive examples of political trials. Even our present-day judges, lawyers, and jurisprudential scholars think of a political trial as evil phenomena fostered by Communists, Third World dictators, or South Africa. Very little thought is given to the idea that there are other sorts of political trials, which are, if properly understood, essential to participating in our political process and, under the right circumstances, help promote justice.

Our book introduces a different idea regarding a political trial, and it presents the argument that political trials are not inherently evil; they can be seen as a positive duty of those holding the public trust. The proposition offered is not that all political trials are justifiable, but rather that different kinds of political trials are justifiable in different kinds of situations. The book is divided into two sections. In the first section, we examine the nature of political trials and debate their cogency. We also consider how they might be justified. In the second section, we examine specific areas of law that are inherently political and at present discriminatory. That is, they work politically to the advantage of certain individuals and groups and oppressively toward others. They distribute social, economic, or political burdens inequitably or embody values that are oppressive. For example, we consider such issues as the bias in favor of Christian religion and how a denial of religious freedom is politically realized, and whether the right to medical care is a fundamental right.

We are happy to thank those many friends who shared with us the thoughts that the subject of political trials inevitably brings to mind. Several people read all or part of earlier drafts and made many valuable suggestions and raised many important criticisms. We are deeply grateful to Jackie Newnam, who once again rescued us from many errors through her patience and devotion in editing and typing the final draft of the manuscript. We also thank the College of Liberal Arts and Sciences at the University of Colorado, Denver, and the Foundation for University Scholarly Publications for their fiscal support.

IN DEFENSE
OF
POLITICAL TRIALS

Chapter One

The Ubiquitous Political Trial

Political trials, contrary to our lawyers, judges, and jurisprudential scholars are not the wicked invention of Fascists and Communists but are respected ways of participating in our political process. In fact, political trials are an indispensable part of our civilization and they work as much justice as we can learn to expect. We might even say that the more political trials we have, the more honestly we can call ourselves a pluralist system dedicated to the greatest good for the greatest number and the protection of individual human rights.

In this book we hope to provide an analytical framework for defining a political trial, what justifies them in certain contexts, and how we might evaluate them to determine when they are the duty of those invested with the public trust. By way of introduction, we will make a few brief points.

It is an inevitable fact of their institutional nature that all courts exercise power through their proceedings. Consequently, any properly running court system cannot avoid exercising this power to stimulate and restrain political change. This is why political trials occur all of the time in every field of law, and this is also why it is so important to distinguish the good ones from the bad ones. To secure our cherished goals and to promote our most fundamental values, each of us sooner or later deals with what the courts have recognized as our rights, duties, and responsibilities and how the courts have prioritized our goals and values with respect to all others.

The need to deal with the court decisions on these priorities and the court definitions of rights and duties never ends. The goals and priorities we think are secure tend to dissolve over time through a case-by-case re-analysis and adjustment in the courts.[1] In the process, the most outrageous ideas often gain ground. It is both the genius and singular fault of the common law that precedents are protean things whose full potential is never understood at their beginnings. Minor changes in circumstance, the vagaries of fortune, or just the passage of time will alter a precedent's meaning and its proper application. Thus, it is always a distinct possibility that the words of any precedent, which secure power or precedence to one person over another, can be so turned as to reverse the situation in the future.

This is why it is such a great temptation to adapt the words of precedent to one's cause and to identify favored ends with a court's prestige. The problem is that once an issue or legal opinion has been politicized, or once some legal device has been used for political ends, it is up for grabs. Sooner or later, a political opponent will use it to turn the tables. Consequently, we cannot pretend that either the law or the courts are above political strife. More often, both are co-opted by one group or must be addressed by another in hopes of making headway in their political cause.

More elaborately, political trials are parleys in what Michel Foucault calls the "dynamic circulation" of social discourse. Though apparently limited to the peculiarities of the case at hand, they are at bottom a form of collective negotiation and exchange among the individuals and groups affected by the different possible outcomes. They are institutionalized procedures for deciding not just the ostensible conflicts among participants but certain issues about the regulation, circulation, distribution, and operation of power as well. They employ a language and type of discourse concerning power that is accepted as authoritative and as a political mechanism through which we can best determine what statements about power are true. In addition, courts are trusted because they function according to techniques and procedures that we have come to value in acquiring truth and in establishing who has the authority and responsibility (the power) to say the truth about power relationships.

These points about the political nature of courts are bolstered by a great deal of empirical evidence and much thoughtful analysis.[2] Courts are created, structured, funded, staffed, and granted jurisdiction by the state. This alone is enough to make the point. In addition, few now dispute the fact that courts are active participants in the political process, and many argue that as participants the courts actively receive demands and authoritatively allocate values.[3] Hence, the act of mobilizing the courts on one's own behalf can sensibly be conceived of as a form of political participation. It has even been hinted, as we shall argue extensively here, that the ability to mobilize the courts adds to the diffusion of power and enhances the democratic nature of our society.[4]

There is also a great deal of evidence and thoughtful analysis supporting the idea that courts cannot help but frustrate or restrict real social change because the understandings and values they bring to bear upon the cases before them reflect the political context in which they are embodied.[5] At the same time, there is equally weighty evidence that interests otherwise restricted or repressed may at least be expressed through litigation and may even gain some support.[6] These last ideas and the bodies of thought behind them are generally understood as offering contradictory views of a court's political role, and the tradition characterizing courts as active participants in the political process rarely goes so far as to suggest that political trials can be not only good things but positive duties as well. Our point, however, is that the previous statements are not contradictory but merely demonstrate (1) that courts reflect their political context and offer points of access for unpopular orientations, and (2) that a properly running court system stimulates and restrains political change and, in the process, must sometimes employ blatantly political trials to fulfill both of these functions.

If we take seriously the political nature of courts and the sociopolitical function of trials as suggested here, we must also take seriously the two important corollaries: First, there must be good as well as bad political trials, and second, what counts as a good or bad political trial must change.

If we think about political trials only in negative terms, for example, restricting our focus to the repressive or prohibitory dimensions of political trials or restricting our use of the term to trials of a repressive or otherwise onerous nature, we will miss most of the discourse that goes on in courts about power, about who has it, and about how it should be distributed. We will miss the larger ensemble of social and institutional practices engaged in and affected by courts that circulate power and constitute the order of things. We will miss most of the struggle among the different networks of relationships that occur on different levels of our society, for example, religion v. state. These networks, which have different breadths, different chronologies, and different ramifications at their own and other levels will nevertheless find their way into our courts in some very interesting ways.

More importantly, if we so restrict our vision, we miss many of the modes of action available through the courts to people in our society who are trying to get, retain, and effectively employ power toward productive ends, we miss the great array of possibilities for resistance and counterattack from all sides upon those holding power; and we will not be able to understand how each gain or offensive by some serves as leverage for others to turn things around. We cannot really understand, for example, how during the eighteenth century the law and the courts became weapons in the struggle against the same monarchical power that had initially made use of both to aggrandize itself by regulating discourse, institutions, and action to produce an order supporting the idea that sovereignty had certain pre-eminent rights.

Trials derive their legitimacy (their evaluations as good or bad) from the cultural functions they serve and from the extent to which they empower or give energy to the pursuit of our goals and the preservation, promotion, and reformulation of our values in the fine web of interpersonal manufacturers, speculators in western lands, and holders of government securities. Agrarian interests were generally placed at a certain disadvantage. Structurally, it supported a strong, centralized, stable, and more coercive national government over the more "democratic" state and locally oriented arrangement that had produced real financial and political problems under the Articles of Confederation. As *The Federalist Papers* (nos. 4, 7, 11, and 12) explains, power was intended to circulate from the top down so that the national government might regulate the political and commercial intercourse among the states and with foreign countries. This centralized regulation was meant partly to prevent and authoritatively resolve disputes among the states and partly to further the national government's ability to open markets and "vivify and invigorate the channels of industry." Of course, one practice supportive of this arrangement was that of discouraging any tendency the press might have to stir things up at the grass-roots level, especially if the news had something bad to say about the national government.

There was nothing necessarily unreasonable, evil, or especially mean about such an order. It certainly circulated power well enough to establish a productive social network yielding substantial amounts of wealth and knowledge. It also ensured that a new nation's stability remained unthreatened by the "great beast" of popular and intergroup struggles. Rarely is this function predominantly repressive or prohibitive. Only under special circumstances are courts justified to say "no." Most often, their function is to make things happen (e.g., property transfers, establishing business entities, contractually defining relationships). Even in those areas in which restriction seems to be the purpose of the law (e.g., regulatory law, criminal law), the briefest examination reveals that the goals and functions of trials are to enhance the operation of what is regulated and the ability of individuals to go safely about their own pursuits.

When trials begin just saying "no"—when they cut short the social discourse—our ability to make things happen declines; our society becomes more wasteful in political, economic, and social terms, and our day-to-day practices begin to encounter unexpected risks, resistances, and loopholes. This happens for two reasons: First, formulating and enforcing prohibitions against change is itself a change in the practices supporting a given order. Thus, trying to preserve order changes it and in the process engenders resistances, risks and loopholes where things would otherwise have run smoothly had there been no change. It is better to promote the discourse and to work out a new, more smoothly functioning order through the resulting collective negotiations. Second, prohibiting an idea or action seems to focus more attention on that which is forbidden and encourages more involvement. Imagine, for example, that you are told about a treasure buried in your back yard. It is yours so long as you do not think of a white monkey. The moment you do have such a thought, the treasure is lost. This simple, direct experiment demonstrates the attention a prohibition engenders, and the speculation and imagination that results. There is simply no way not to think about something when it is suggested to you, and as you think about it, you also imagine the possibilities. It also demonstrates the inducement to do what you are not supposed to do, especially if you think you do not want to do it. This is where risk, resistance, and loophole begin.

In other words, whether a trial fulfills its sociopolitical/economic functions, whether it is a positive use of power, or whether it operates to effectively circulate power or to just say "no" determines whether it is political and whether it is good or bad. Of course, this means that to determine what counts as a political trial (e.g., to determine if such a charge is true) and then to evaluate the truth of any charge that any given political trial is good or bad, we must not employ a standard derived from our own model of the way things work and the correct function of trials in the current milieu (i.e., the current distribution of power relationships and the rules concerning the nature of those relationships). Rather, we must grasp the meaning of the trial in terms of the people involved. How do trials function in their social, political, economic, and individual strategies, tactics, and techniques for getting things done?

All of this is a bit abstract but will become more concrete as we study how courts have actually acted in good, bad, repressive, and facilitative ways in different historical contexts. By way of illustration, though, let's briefly consider a few cases involving freedom of the press. Freedom of the press is a potent political tool in our society that is capable of breaking political candidates and unmaking elected presidents. It is doubtful whether either the scandal over candidate Gary Hart's sexual escapades in the 1988 presidential race or the Watergate investigation of the Nixon presidency would have been possible had the Supreme Court not articulated the "Sullivan Rule." Under that rule, the press is protected against libel verdicts in favor of public officials unless the press report at issue was not only false and damaging but made with "actual malice." Carelessness or even negligent research is not enough. The media must either know its report is false or "recklessly disregard" its truth or falsity. Consequently, an industry has been made of the practice of doing extensive research with the explicit intent of uncovering the merest whiff of unsavory behavior by public figures.

Now, what is interesting for our purposes is that the Sullivan case represents a change in our "discursive regime." The Supreme Court, through Justice William Brennan's opinion, used the words of the First Amendment in ways that meant something different than had been meant before. The premises of the First Amendment were redefined and more than libel law was affected as a result. One effect was to free the press from the need to constantly defend itself in court where a jury might seize on some factual mistake or journalist's imprecision to award a bankrupting verdict. The Court's explicit purpose in issuing the Sullivan Rule was to increase the likelihood of more informed choices by the electorate. It sought to do this by increasing the dynamic circulation of social discourse throughout the entire social web and by reducing the risks to the institutions facilitating such circulation and the possible modes of resistance available to those interested in restricting such circulation. This, in turn, effectively changed the whole ensemble of social practices supporting the extant power relationships among officials, journalists, candidates, individual members of the public, and the public at large.

It is worth noting that although the Sullivan case significantly redefines certain power relationships within our society, it is not oppressive, prohibitory, or especially onerous to the losers. No one is punished for bringing suit; it is simply harder to prevail. The power of public officials wanes, but they are not debarred or repressed. Yet, to deny the political nature of this case is to studiously ignore what we understand about politics and power. There is no question, for example, that the Court changed the law with the Sullivan case rather than simply drawing out the necessary implications of the law or "legislating in the interstices."

Historically, the language of the free press guarantee has offered an especially effective opportunity for employing the courts as a mode of resistance to the discursive regime supporting a given ensemble of practices (i.e., a given order). As we will detail later, most Americans in 1798 understood the free press guarantee as a right against previous restraint. The government could not prevent the publication of anything but it could punish offensive or dangerous publications after the fact. This understanding was embedded and circulated in a discursive regime of its own—a set of verbal practices employed during trials and used in writing judicial decisions that supported a certain order and a certain way of making power circulate through that order so that things could happen.

Substantively, this discourse and the legal decisions cast in its terms favored business interests, agitation—a beast whose voraciousness had been witnessed during the French Revolution. But in an attempt to preserve this order from any grass-roots change, the established power structure produced the Sedition Act, which made it a crime to publish anything "false, scandalous or malicious" about members of Congress or the president. Suppressing those critical of the government by making them face the possibility of ruinous fines or imprisonment pushed an important sector of the American public to the fringes of the power web. It effectively left small freehold farmers out of the collective negotiations about power—who should have it and how it should be used.

Inevitably, this produced resistance and such risks as could only be met by force and repression by the courts. In 1794, for example, President George Washington sent 13,000 militiamen against a few farmers in open revolt against a federal tax on whiskey. Privately, he ascribed this rebellion to subversive forces and opined that "democratic societies" should be exterminated. In this context, the Sedition Act was used to indict, fine, or imprison Republican (Antifederalist) writers and publishers for criticizing the president and his administration. As the Antifederalists quickly realized, however, these prosecutions laid not only the government but the financial and political order open to attack in the language of liberty and human rights, and they promised to turn the courts around from a mode of enforcing the order to a mode of resistance. Jefferson, in particular, provided an alternative discursive regime to the Federalists and so managed to use the risks posed by the Sedition Act as leverage for a counteroffensive in the courts. Basically, he argued that the Federalist government had exceeded its powers when it passed a law ordering punishment for what people might say. Such a law, Jefferson argued, constituted the denial of a freedom guaranteed by the Constitution regardless of whether there was any prior restraint.

Here began a new meaning of the free press language that was not to become orthodox until the 1960s, when dissents in certain cases decided under the Espionage Act of World War I were adopted by the Supreme Court as defining the new discursive regime. Justice Holmes's dissent in *Abrams v. U.S.*,[7] was particularly useful in this regard. Holmes's opinion declared that our Constitution committed us to an "experiment" testing truth by "the power of the thought to get itself accepted in the competition of the market," and that only such speech as presented a "clear and present danger" to society could be punished. His dissent provided the discursive opportunity for civil rights advocates, labor unions, and antiwar protestors to employ courts in changing the ensemble of practices supporting the political, economic, and social order that left them with risky and inefficient means of exercising power that were full of loopholes.

We see in this brief example the dynamic tension that exists among groups and individuals over how power circulates in society, as well as the shifting of national posture that can occur as the institutions of government focus first on using courts to control certain groups under a given order and then on responding to those same groups once they manage to successfully employ the courts as a mode of resistance and then as a support for a different order. We also see how a given order can go too far, becoming too controlling (repressive) or too responsive (disintegrating). In response to Jefferson's discursive alternative, for example, Kentucky passed a set of resolutions in 1799 proclaiming the right of states to nullify unconstitutional acts of Congress. Jefferson quickly disavowed this and similar resolutions in Virginia, rejecting the doctrine of nullification as likely to endanger the union.

Since these ideas are so important for understanding and evaluating political trials, we need to take a closer look at how they are embodied in the day-to-day workings of our courts. Once we understand how the courts function as a co-equal branch of government, stimulating and restraining change, we can explicate why political trials are sometimes justified and the duty of those who govern.

POLITICAL TRIALS AND THE FUSION OF FUNCTIONS

Our legislative, executive, and judicial branches of government engage in some functions formally assigned to the other. This is necessary because the executive and judicial branches must establish rules with legal effect if they are to carry out congressional mandates. It is also necessary because Congress must hold hearings and have the power to direct sanctions if it is to act as an effective check against the executive and the judiciary. Similarly, the delegation of judicial and legislative functions to the regulatory arm of the executive branch is usually necessary because of the specialized nature of the regulated activity (placing it beyond the general competency of the legislature and judiciary), and because regulatory agencies are usually charged either with developing and implementing solutions to rapidly arising problems or regulating ongoing activities. Neither the congressional nor judicial branches can consistently react with the speed necessary under such circumstances. They must be content to review the policies of regulatory agencies and keep them generally within the bounds of due process.

Such fusion of functions is not only necessary but proper because it does not obliterate the separation of powers, which is still preserved through the process of review. Governmental authority is dispersed to prevent absolutism, and political safeguards are kept in place to defend against the capricious exercise of power.

The fusion is also proper because one major drawback to strict separation is overcome. Because separation of powers encourages the executive, the legislative, and the judiciary to move in independent spheres, the programs they support and pursue often work at cross-purposes. Coherent policy is therefore difficult to create, and important policies are often legislated piecemeal, enforced sporadically or too quickly, and are always subject to judicial revision. As policies falter and crises develop, one branch or another must step forward to fill the gap. Often this is the president, which has resulted in our idea of "the imperial presidency." But at other times, it is the judiciary, as was the case in the late sixties when the president was beleaguered by public opinion against the Vietnam War and oscillating congressional support. Separation of powers, then, often means that one branch can act when the others are frozen, even if its activity is not strictly within the formal limits set by the separation of powers doctrine.

So our political institutions have a mixed character, each branch incorporating aspects of the functions and the powers of the others. Politics and law are thus inevitably and properly mixed. On balance, this fusion constitutes a productive network running through the entire government, making things happen and facilitating discourse among the branches and between the government and the populace. This network increases efficiency by
 loopholes that would otherwise persist under the strict separationist
linking the public to the government at many points and

in many ways (such as the local, state, and federal courthouses). Because of this network and the access it provides, events (e.g., decisions, policy making, rule making) in the different branches and events of all sorts in the society at large can ramify throughout the government, hopefully evoking the proper, balanced mix of responses from different decision makers, committees, elected officials, and functionaries. In brief, this fusion is a technique allowing power to circulate more efficiently and less wastefully.

As we will illustrate, however, it is in the nature of power relationships to make things work at times too efficiently or inefficiently, if at all. The courts, for example, have at times been too quick to move in seeking the demise of certain vague dangers. On the other hand, they have at times been either frustrated by other, more tangible threats. This inertia, this displacement of power onto undeserving objects and this resistance to the circulation of power reflect the multiple, dispersed, and heteromorphous nature of power and result from the variety of forms that power relationship can take.

Fusion can also encourage certain biases because our political ideal of separation of powers fosters a respect for the law as being above politics. Court rulings tend to legitimate legislative and executive policies in the mind of the general public (after all, if such policies were wrong, the court would strike them down; if the policies are struck down, the government is back on track again and so legitimate). At the same time, courts are part of our governmental structure and, thus, inevitably drawn into politics as instruments of political conflict. For example, "The fact that criminal courts are populated mostly by the poor while civil courts are used principally by middle class citizens raises the question for some people whether a ruling elite uses the courts to oppress the disadvantaged."[8] Similarly, courts can reflect the biases of politically predominant groups, as they often do, by favoring the rights of property owners, religious institutions, and certain political groups (e.g., conservatives, liberals, and even fascists) over others (e.g., Communists).

Although courts may sometimes act as biased arbiters championing the causes of certain groups and legitimating those causes as expressions of our highest ideals, our society really works in such a way that neither their wandering from popular attitudes and habits nor their oppression of particular groups is forever tolerated (though gradual, case-by-case reinterpretations of our attitudes have the effect of re-educating us slowly). There have been some interesting studies of exactly how this works.[9] They tend to demonstrate that while court decisions do legitimate, they also solidify and activate opposition groups. The court's decision increases an issue's salience, reprioritizing the goals of many groups, and the court's reasoning gives special interest groups something palpable to work with, consider, answer, and defend. Thus, should the courts go too far against such ideals as freedom and equality, for example, they will undoubtedly be reminded of their proper place first by the populace (e.g., the public reaction by northerners to the Dred Scott decision in the last century, and this century's resistance by many southern school districts to the "no prayer in public schools" decision), and then by those of the executive and legislative branches eager to garner public support (e.g., the court-packing attempt by Franklin Roosevelt in the 1930s).

In addition, the law employed by courts has a certain logic of its own. Law has its own characteristics and history, its own methods and ideals, which is independent of the history of particular groups. This independence prevents it from becoming too pliant a medium to be simply twisted every which way for political ends.

Overall, then, our law is grounded in our "form of life" (our characteristic patterns of interaction, values expectations, orientations, and the character of our social institutions), which in this civilization is a decidedly political struggle among groups and individuals over the distribution of wealth, power, and the right to define what constitutes a good, productive, and valuable human being. Courts can never be free of this struggle and were, in fact, created to help manage the competition through the exercise of power as a co-equal branch, which is responsive to political reality and inured with a certain integrity of its own. This brings us to the protean nature of power and its use to effect political ends in every field of law.

POWER, POLITICAL TRIALS, AND CRIMINAL LAW

Everybody knows that criminal trials are often political. They understand that people are harassed, imprisoned, and persecuted by criminal charges creatively applied to unpopular causes. They also understand that this is often what legislatures intend when they pass vague statutes affecting sensitive and fundamental individual and social rights. All of this is somewhat unremarkable to us because it can be demonstrated historically that such a use of the criminal law is an important and popular American tradition.

Fairly recent examples include two imaginative uses of conspiracy charges against anti-Vietnam War activists in the 1970s. The trial of the "Chicago Seven" for conspiring to cross state lines to commit a riot was prosecuted against seven defendants apparently selected to "represent the varying components of what has been called 'the new left'."[10] Similarly, the "prosecution of Dr. Benjamin Spock and his co-defendants for conspiracy to counsel selective service registrants to evade military service was apparently brought to silence the dissemination of information the government found it inconvenient for the general populace to have."[11] An earlier example was the Korean War prosecution of John William Powell for publishing a variety of stories substantiating, detailing, and documenting Chinese and North Korean charges that the United States was engaging in germ warfare.[12] This occurred at about the same time in the 1950s that the states were busy riddling their criminal codes with well over 300 astonishingly harsh and now clearly unconstitutional enactments aimed at "subversive activities."[13]

We find similar uses of the criminal trial at the turn of this century. First there was the various conspiracy charges brought against prominent political figures under the First World War's Espionage Act.[14] Then there was the criminal prosecutions aimed at the burgeoning labor movement, including the Industrial Workers of the World[15] and Chicago's anarcho-communists.[16] Earlier still were the summary arrests, military detentions, and military trials of "all persons discouraging volunteer enlistments" under Lincoln's proclamations of executive law during the Civil War,[17] and following independence in 1776, we find the Alien and Sedition Act prosecutions of Jeffersonian editors and congressmen, followed quickly by the prosecution of Federalist sympathizers by the Jeffersonians.[18] Finally, in the very misty beginnings, before we were even a nation, we find the unabashed prosecution of newspaper editors Thomas Greenleaf and William Corbett for criminal libel and contempt after they printed insults aimed at the British and Spanish ambassadors, respectively.[19]

Of course, the evils attendant to such criminal trials are so glaring and so inexcusable that many are now focused singularly upon the potential abuse of criminal law for political ends. But while there is nothing wrong with this focus, it is simply out of date. The criminal law is no longer the primary jurisprudential tool for oppressive political ends. Civil law does just as well if it is properly used, as do administrative and regulatory law, military law, equity, and even the regulations of private judicial bodies. We need to understand all of this if we are to understand our society as it exists today. That is, we need to understand at least how oppressive political trials originate as events in the different types of networks at the different levels of society. We then need to understand how those networks are affected in turn and how the different power relationships in our society are affected by the chronologies of the decisions (i.e., the times at which the decisions occur and the "lifespans" of the decisions before they are overturned, ignored, or distinguished away). If we understand how power circulates within and among these networks, we can understand who is being served by oppressive political trials and how the power circulating through the courts can be used to work a positive political change. As we have said, one justification of political trials is that they hold just such a promise of being positively as well as negatively used; and once this is accomplished, the judicial branch makes a special contribution to democratic government.

Amiable people might point out that all of the legal devices just mentioned are thoroughly well intentioned. They might say, for example, that administrative law protects us against the overreach of our government's regulation; that regulatory law protects us against the egregious negligences and depredations of one another and the major concentrations of capital in our society; that civil law facilitates personal decision making and rational choice by regularizing expectations and securing interpersonal transactions; that equity provides a needed leavening to ensure that justice is done when the strict formalities of law fall short; that private judicial bodies provide a social option to the often blind judicial system; and that military law is absolutely necessary to deal with the peculiarities of that curious institution. In short, they might say that ours is meant to be a government of laws shielding us from political, social, and economic oppression, that these laws are enforced and enacted by well-meaning people of good will, and that most of us get along under these laws without unbearable discontent.

Against such an opinion, it is undeniably slack to argue that well-meaning people of good will are as prone to the ruthless pursuit of bad policy when they are mistaken, as they are to the avid pursuit of good policy when they are correct; that the good a law does as often comes about despite its operation as because of it; or that the real criterion of a law is not how well we persevere under it but how well we flourish. Rather, we must establish that the devices of civil law, administrative law, regulatory law, military law, equity, and private judicial regulation are, in fact, commonly employed for oppressive political ends, thereby establishing not only all of the points just made, but the ubiquity of political trials as well. Not only that, but as we have introduced the hope that these same devices might be otherwise more positively employed, we bear some burden of substantiating this as well. Therefore, we are going to take each of these devices and examine their political potential.

POLITICAL TRIALS AND CIVIL LAW

Civil law is a great boon to society, but we must remember that it was largely the failures of civil law that made politically necessary not only those most idiosyncratic of legal devices, regulatory and administrative law, but that most nettlesome of social devices, the union. In addition, the failures of civil law, and more particularly its use for political ends, engendered necessary political responses in the legislatures and the courts.

Consider, for example, the case of *Thornton and Wife v. The Suffolk Manufacturing Company.*[20] It had long been the custom in Lowell, Massachusetts, not to hire anyone from another factory who did not possess a written letter of "honorable discharge." Usually, these letters were written if the employee had "faithfully performed her duties" for a period of at least twelve months. This practice had been fastidiously adhered to by every company representative who testified in the case and had been followed with the strictest punctilio for at least five years prior to the disagreement at issue.

Nevertheless, in the summer of 1849, Catherine Cassidy was discharged without the necessary paper from the Suffolk Manufacturing Company after twelve months of fine work, fine to the point of being rewarded by the company with special training in the art of weaving. Now the company's agent said "she might come back [to the same plant], assured her that she was a very good girl, and that there was nothing against her."[21] But Catherine wanted to work elsewhere, found it completely impossible to do so without the letter, and sued for breach of contract. She argued that granting such a letter was an implied term of her employment with the Suffolk Manufacturing Company.

The court found no contract, held that had such a contract been expressly made it would have been "bad in law as contrary to good morals and public policy,"[22] and ruled that as a matter of law the issuance of such a paper was entirely within the discretion of the company.[23] Clearly, the civil law was employed in *Thornton* to exercise and affirm capital's power over labor. In this way, it was a distinctly political trial, engendering organized labor, collective bargaining, and the Wagner Act over the next eighty years.

Of course, those who exercise private authority through the civil law are not exclusively nor even largely our employers. And the response to such political uses of the courts come just as often from the courts themselves as from the legislative branch. Our society is crisscrossed with perplexing power hierarchies, and the civil law has been employed in the courts to affect every personal interface.

An interesting series of cases from North Carolina registers this interplay. *Joyner v. Joyner*[24] was an 1862 case of a wife petitioning for divorce because her husband beat her with a horsewhip. Citing Biblical precedent (Gen. 3:16), the court denied the petition, deciding that "the wife must be subject to the husband. Every man must govern his household."[25] Thus, the court enforced a certain power relationship within the family.

Two years later, the court extended this holding to include a husband and wife living apart,[26] and four years later, it reaffirmed *Joyner*, when a husband beat his wife with a switch "no bigger than his thumb." But in this last case, the court hedged a bit by saying that the court would not interfere "with family government in trifling cases."[27] And with that hedge, things began to turn. Seizing on this last phrase, the court in 1870 held that swinging at the wife with a knife was not a trifling matter,[28] and twelve years after *Joyner*, the court held, in *State v. Oliver*, that no general rule of judicial intervention would be applied; each case would be considered on its merits.[29] Thus, the husband's power, once of biblical proportions, was rendered ambiguous, and a wife might hope to wield the courts on her behalf.

Women might not see sufficient progress in all of this to warrant a sigh of relief, but for our present purposes, it is clear enough that these cases were not about assault, battery, attempted murder, or even spousal incompatibility. They were about the protection of established authority and the maintenance of hierarchical relationships, and it is also clear that civil law did manage to accomplish some modest waning of a husband's once absolute power within the family.

So, civil law has a history of use in maintaining and altering the balance of power between those seeking change and those in a position to resist it. Of course, reasonable people may differ over whether the trials just mentioned were political (we will deal with these reasonable disagreements in the next chapter), and for that reason we must look to the federal government for an indisputably political trial in the civil courts. This was accomplished in *Snepp v. U.S.*,[30] in which the CIA contrived to silence critics of its Vietnam chicanery by suing one of its own for breach of contract.

When hired by the CIA, Frank W. Snepp agreed "not . . . to publish . . . any information or material relating to the agency, its activities generally, either during or after the term of employment . . . without specific prior approval by the agency."[31] He then published *Decent Interval*, a book detailing malfeasance and corruption in the CIA during the U.S. withdrawal from South Vietnam. Though all of the material was already published in different places (Snepp's contribution was to gather it together and focus it on a theme), and none of it was classified, the court found a breach of contract, imposed a constructive trust on Snepp's profits, enjoined him from speaking or writing about the CIA for the rest of his life, and fined him $140,000.

Agreeable and tolerant people might wrangle over the substantiveness of the breach, the damage to the CIA, and the propriety of the remedy. Sharper people might inquire as to whether there was a breach at all, or whether the contract was "bad in law as plainly contrary to good morals and public policy."[32] But no ordinary person can avoid the insight that this case is not so much about breaching a contract as it is about punishing people who criticize the government.

The CIA was so principled as to declare this openly on several occasions. The first was when CIA Director Richard Helms, testifying in another case, listed three people who to his knowledge published articles without agency approval and were not prosecuted.[33] Next, at the district court level of Snepp's prosecution, CIA witnesses testified that they did not require CIA officers to submit material for prepublication review.[34] This was repeated at the appellate court level, along with a CIA admission that two books and "a number of articles" were published by former employees without prepublication review as required by the secrecy agreement, and without action being taken to prevent or punish the violation.[35] Finally, the CIA testified before Congress that it selectively enforced the review requirement solely to silence critics.[36]

The court, however, would tolerate no recourse to the defenses of selective prosecution of First Amendment guarantees. This was a civil case. Snepp had signed a contract defining the legal relationship between himself and the CIA and the agreement had been voluntary.[37] Thus, even though a statute requiring such an agreement and attaching a criminal sanction for its violation would not have passed constitutional muster,[38] and even though the selective enforcement of such a statute would have constituted a sufficient defense to its violation, because the CIA brought a civil prosecution, Snepp was simply out of luck.[39] The lesson is that although the government cannot suppress criticism by statute, it can do so by contract.

So far, we have invoked the unpleasant specter of the government and private citizens using civil law to run rampant over civil and human rights. Consider, however, the following case, similar to *Snepp*, which not only illustrates that there are good political trials and that they are sometimes a duty but also serves as a transition to our discussion about political trials and regulatory law.

Philip Agee had also signed the secrecy oath made infamous by *Snepp*, but Agee published classified material, material not published before, and material exposing the identities and activities of CIA operatives abroad. He did this all in a frank attempt to destroy CIA networks involved in what he reviled as "military coups, torture, and terrorism."[40]

Now, the CIA is not involved in a noble business, and we often pay the price of its brutishness through lost allies and political defeats. But Agee, like many Americans, believed that wrongs may be righted by independent displays of coercive self-righteousness. He forgot, as many of us do, that within our society our idea of justice results not by personal and private crusades but by popular and public campaigns aimed at educating, persuading, cajoling, enticing, and charming people and politicians into legislating and enforcing the necessary rules and regulations.

The needed restraint on CIA cruelty (and all other governmental chicanery) that Agee clearly perceived was necessary according to our traditional values, must, according to those values, be first and last a matter of law— probably a whole structure of laws striking that balance between virtue and effectiveness that is what we understand to be the delicate goal of good government. In our society, virtue, such as Agee's, is at best politically useless and more often socially destructive without laws and institutions to give it practical meaning. While people charged with a public trust may not always fulfill their responsibilities to virtue, private individuals taking upon themselves a private responsibility for public virtue risk damaging the productive power networks running through our society and produce only disorder. This sometimes makes repression necessary and often produces unavoidable political trials. The trick for governments at such times is to be only so repressive as to re-establish the context within which virtue can be publicly (i.e., socially) pursued. Of course, it is sometimes difficult for government to display this moderation; and then we must have civil disobedience. But, as we shall see, this is different than personal self-righteousness. Properly done, civil disobedience might reconstitute or refurbish productive networks corrupted by bad government and so contribute to overall stability.

Given that the CIA richly deserved a legal thrashing, Agee simply set out to smash it himself. Consequently, the federal government had no choice but to prosecute him and to halt the clearly predictable havoc he would wreak. The problem was that the Justice Department could find no grounds for prosecuting him under the Espionage Act,[41] and since Agee insisted on traveling and publishing abroad, the CIA could not get him into court for breach of contract. So the Secretary of State revoked his passport. Agee immediately sued the secretary for violating his rights to travel and to criticize the government, and because the government could produce no statute making Agee's activities a ground for passport revocation, the trial and appellate courts ordered the secretary to reinstate the passport.[42]

The Supreme Court was less solicitous. It saw beyond the rules of law to the human facts of the case and drew a boundary around Agee's rights to speech and travel. The Court's decision was certainly political: It circumscribed rights clearly recognized in law so that the political interests of the United States might be furthered and maintained; it redefined the balance of power between citizens and the government and between those seeking to bring about change and those in a position to resist it; and it intimated, chillingly, that First Amendment protections do not reach beyond the nation's boundaries.[43] In short, the court did everything in *Agee* that it did in *Snepp*; but unlike *Snepp*, *Agee* was not really a disguised case about criticizing the government. It was about removing a direct, serious threat of physical harm to U.S. agents abroad, avoiding palpable injury to proper national interests, and curtailing an intentional misuse of privileged information to cause these absolutely predictable results. Consequently, this political trial was justifiable and the duty of those entrusted with the public good.

Unfortunately, the Court tried to make this all clear by enlisting that quaint obfuscation that words can somehow have the force of physical acts (i.e., by announcing that speech and dangerous conduct are sometimes the same). This was unfortunate because while this idea is steeped in tradition, it is most often employed to justify the repression of legitimate dissent. Consequently, it engenders much concern about where the court is going with regard to First Amendment rights and casts a pall over an otherwise just decision.

Justice Holmes, for example, found some dangerous words in a newspaper's accusation that the government was guilty of murder for sending American troops to France during the First World War.[44] As he said, "It is impossible to say that it might not have been found that the circulation of the newspaper was in quarters where a little breath would be enough to kindle a flame and that the fact was known and relied upon by those who sent the paper out."[45] But these words, probably understood by their maker as a defense of the national interest in a unique situation, have been used for oppressive political ends to such an extent that we are forever being alerted to the substantial risk of evil we run if "properly deranged minds" are sparked by seemingly innocent words.[46] The words of this precedent have been turned around and used to attack people rather than defend them. Thus, they have accomplished much political mischief and produced many a bad political trial.

How this occurred is not really difficult to understand. This sort of talk is really metaphor, not argument, and while proper metaphors can enhance an argument, used by themselves they can stir our emotions to the point of driving us past reason and into mere reaction. Rationally speaking, for example, it seems that properly deranged minds might get the necessary incitement from nonsense syllables as easily as from the *Communist Manifesto*. Besides, if we start making policy with the properly deranged mind in view, we have effectively written off the First Amendment. But the vision of some unknown political fanatic driven to terrorism by the passion of political beliefs stirred by some metaphorical argument to which more rational minds are impervious becomes especially scary when its possibility is validated by a justice of the Supreme Court.

So, the image of sparks, breath, and fire has served historically to sustain decisions oppressing dissident newspapers, speeches, and organizations,[47] and the fear of properly deranged minds has facilitated the venting of judicial ire on some silly, although thoroughly harmless, conduct. In 1792, for example, Luther Borden was convicted of sedition for mentioning, in a drunken stupor, that he wished a cannon to be fired at the president's posterior. Similarly, in 1966 John Pierce was convicted after a display of bravado, designed to impress a drunken cellmate, led him to ask his jailers to mail a threatening letter, scrawled on the back of an envelope, to the president.[48]

Given this history, it might have been much better to simply admit in the *Agee* case that the First Amendment is not relevant in those unique situations in which the sane reason, thoughtful reflection, and sound argument of those at whom the speech is aimed must result (because it is their duty) in direct and immediate physical harm to specific U.S. agents and interests abroad. But perhaps this is not really a better way. The idea that the First Amendment is sometimes irrelevant might be more damaging, should it catch on, than the idea that words and not people start fires.

More stentorian political trials than these are seldom found outside criminal law. But we can find quieter ones, and interestingly enough, they often revolve around the regulation of speech. When the state decides to oversee some behavior on an ongoing basis, it is regulating it, as opposed to outlawing, even though it may use the criminal sanction to enforce its regulation.

Commercial speech is one example. Words are required for commercial activity and knowing we need something often depends on someone telling us it is available. Commercial speech is regulated to keep people from lying to us, misleading us, or encouraging us to engage in unlawful activity.[49]

This presents an interesting puzzle. If words encouraging unlawful activity are unlawful, and if unlawful utterances are not protected by the Constitution, then any government (state or federal) can escape the operation of free speech guarantees by making any class of commercial activity unlawful. At least it is worth a try.

Consider, for example, what happened when the *Virginia Weekly* began advertising out-of-state abortion counseling and abortion referral services.[50] This activity violated a Virginia statute making it unlawful to encourage or prompt the procuring of an abortion by the sale or circulation of any publication. Making it unlawful to "encourage or prompt" abortion was of course read broadly to make illegal the imparting of information on where, how, and when to obtain abortions; an unabashed attempt to frustrate the exercise of a recognized (though not entirely popular) constitutional right to an abortion as delineated in *Roe v. Wade*.[51] Still, Virginia hoped to skirt an obvious challenge to the law's constitutionality by arguing that such information was not constitutionally protected because it promoted unlawful activity.

The Supreme Court was not amused. Ruling that Virginia had no legitimate interest in keeping this particular information from its citizens, the Court, in *Bigelow v. Virginia*, limited slightly the power of states to create crimes in the regulation of commercial speech. This deftly frustrated certain state attempts to get around the Constitution, but the holding in the case was so narrowly drawn that it did not constitute a clear signal to the states that they might never use this approach to circumvent the First Amendment or prohibit private conduct they find immoral.

Cases making the narrowness of this limitation clear include *Princess Sea Industries v. State*, which held that a state may prohibit advertising prostitution where it is legal in some counties but illegal in others,[52] and *Dunigan v. City of Oxford*, which held the same for alcoholic beverages.[53] *Bigelow* can be distinguished from these last cases because the right to terminate a pregnancy is fundamental,[54] while the rights to consume alcoholic beverages and visit prostitutes are not—at this time.

Once there was no fundamental right to an abortion; it was not a subject of regulation; it was a crime. Things were changed through social and political agitation, some of which involved illegal activity, much of which was hard to avoid given how our system works as it moves toward something more than incremental change. Had the state curtailed speech about this illegal activity because it might promote or encourage it, change might have been severely retarded. Moreover, the likelihood of violence and self-help, along the lines of *Agee* may have been greatly increased.

Let's take a look at a more contemporary example for purposes of illustration. At present there is no fundamental right to choose one's sexual orientation. Our courts do not say this directly. Rather, they say that states may discriminate against gays and may prohibit homosexual erotic practices. The Supreme Court does not say anything. It simply refuses to review lower court rulings on the constitutionality of these prohibitions and discriminations, leaving it to the individual states, some finding a fundamental right[55] and some not really looking for one.[56]

To change this state of affairs under our system, gays have to organize, stay organized, and grow continuously in their organizational sophistication. Organizing thus clearly implies that gays must be who they are openly. Responsible social movement aimed at changing institutions, accepted ways of living, and the laws going along with them first requires changing the way people behave on a day-to-day basis.

In other words, the ensemble of practices supporting a particular order must first be changed. To do that and to set up a network of relationships to concentrate and transmit the social power of any set of individuals, you must advertise. You must let people know that there are other people among whom certain behaviors are accepted and from whom support for a social movement might be had. But more importantly, people must do what they did not do before, regularize their behavior into a habit, thus taking its naturalness as an unremarkable assumption. This involves organizing and advertising any opportunity for such behavior on an ongoing basis.

Imagine now that a gay rights organization in a state where homosexual activity is not prohibited advertises marriage and vacation packages for gays in a state prohibiting the "encouraging or prompting of homosexuality by the sale or circulation of any publication." Since the advertisement is speech promoting an illegal activity (the encouraging of homosexuality), and since what has been made illegal does not bear upon a fundamental right, the state could probably ban it and abort the responsible and civilized process of social change. As a result, homosexuality is never recognized as a fundamental right because it did not have the protections guaranteed to a fundamental right before people became sufficiently motivated to see if enough support for its recognition could be garnered from those most directly concerned.

This is clearly contrary to a system of ordered procedures for the regulation and circulation of statements and not what we understand to be good government. Of course, support may never be forthcoming and if it is, the wider society might still veto the issue. But it is the opportunity to put a way of life to the political and social test that is important. And it is that opportunity that may be chilled through regulation.

The political potential of regulatory law is probably clear from this example. But just to drive the point home, let's consider another, this time involving some regulatory authority delegated to the executive. In 1975, the FBI reported an end to its congressionally authorized Programme of Planning for "the emergency arrest and summary detention" of American citizens,[57] which had been in operation for thirty-six years. Enemy lists for the same purposes had been regularly kept under different congressional pronouncements since at least 1798.[58] But what started in 1798 as an authorization to investigate, arrest, and deport enemy aliens during times of war expanded over time to include (1) investigating, arresting, and deporting naturalized citizens in times of peace, (2) the summary arrest and detention of anyone either about to engage in disloyal practices or who did, or would probably, engage in subversive speech or affiliation, (3) the keeping of "custodial detention lists" of people thought to be engaged in pro-Castro Cuban activities, (4) the investigation of all members of every commune, and (5) the investigation of any person from whom any interference with the effective operation of the national, state, or local government could be expected, regardless of affiliation.[59]

Different legal procedures were, of course, developed for different situations. Deportation, for example, required notice, fair hearing, and bail.[60] Likewise, arrests under a 1948 plan for the summary arrest of all dangerous persons in times of emergency, required a master arrest warrant and hearings before special "Boards of Review."[61] Nevertheless, deportations could occur under that plan without criminal charges and could result even though a citizen could not be sanctioned by a regular court of law for the same behavior. Moreover, the 1948 Boards of Review were not bound by the normal rules of evidence, and there was neither recourse to the courts nor appeal except to the president. Generally, all of these delegations of regulatory power to the executive branch "politicized" the exercise of law by removing the procedures normally available for a meaningful defense and expanding the discretion of administrative officials.

It is not difficult to be sympathetic with politicizing the law in this way, even though the wrongheadedness of such delegations is understood. We must, after all, protect and preserve the institutions and way of life from which have come such great discoverers, inventors, pioneers, scientists, moralists, missionaries, Olympic champions, and capital financiers. Our periodic bouts of mutual self-congratulation are not all humbug. We have produced great wealth and liberty and these need defending. But these extraordinary people and their great accomplishments do not always receive encouragement from our institutions or way of life. Often they are resisted and sharply rebuked, and in the process, formal restraints on our political institutions are relaxed.

The history of summary arrest and detention in America, for example, clearly demonstrates how easily a patriotic concern for preserving our institutions sweeps everything before it and breaks down every constitutional barrier. In its ceaseless search for subversion, our patriotism has suspended the writ of *habeas corpus*,[62] and swooped down on "radical hangouts," arresting everyone in sight[63] (including the entire cast and audience of a play performed by Ukranians, and some thirty-nine bakers meeting to discuss the formation of a co-operative).[64] It has bugged, shadowed, and burglarized critical congressmen;[65] engaged in the systematic, forced evacuation and subsequent incarceration of thousands of citizens;[66] provided master arrest warrants and blanket search warrants;[67] halted jury trials, forbidden cross examination, forbidden the confrontation of adverse witnesses, and forbidden the right of appeal.[68]

Patriotism, of course, is not the problem. It is mindless, undirected, and uncontrolled patriotic activity that gets us into trouble. The problem with the sort of hearings provided under summary arrest and detention, for example, is that while they are strongly directed at the punishment of subversion, and while they resolve ambiguity, settle questions, and reduce frustration, fear, and doubt, they are liable to strike anyone at any time. Without the usual guarantees of counsel, *habeas corpus*, notice, juries, cross-examinations, and appeals, the power of our government is completely uncontrolled. While some argue that it is sometimes best to function without thought or understanding, in the long run civilized government depends on an intelligent control of the state's coercive power. State activity is positively mischievous without careful direction and constant control.

Fortunately, regulatory trials can sometimes be used to stir up the kind of controlled activity we are talking about; this is the positive political use of regulatory law. At the turn of this century, the National Consumer's League was deftly at work getting labor legislation passed and enforced at the state level.[69] This was passionately resisted in the courts as contrary to public morality and the Constitution. The league responded with the "Brandeis Brief," which contained a few pages of legal argument and a deluge of social and economic evidence on the impact of the regulation and its nonenforcement or absence.[70] While not uniformly successful, the brief's effects were profound and, in conjunction with a number of other legal and political strategies, contributed heavily to the successful enforcement and defense of regulations aimed at working conditions, wages, hours, and child welfare. This was, of course, a revolution—a revolution controlled by law and directed by a social and economic need that had been well documented by the disciplined activity and research of civilized social activists properly employing the courts politically.

EQUITY AND THE POLITICAL TRIAL

The law of equity is a rather elaborate system of jurisprudence affording relief where courts of law cannot because what the parties deserve cannot be measured in money. Courts of equity thus provide special remedies, one of which is the injunction. Injunctions stop people from doing things that would cause irreparable harm and that are not recompensable by a suit for damages after the fact. At the same time, injunctions are powerful political weapons. The California courts, for example, once brought the Industrial Workers of the World (IWW) to a dead stop by issuing a temporary injunction ordering them to

absolutely desist . . . from further conspiring to . . . take over and assume possession
of the industries . . . and circulating, selling, distributing, and displaying books, pamphlets, papers or other written or printed matter teaching or suggesting criminal
syndicalism or otherwise advocating its necessity or propriety . . . and from organizing
or aiding to organize or increase any assemblage or association of persons which
teaches . . . criminal syndicalism . . . as a means of accomplishing a change in industrial
ownership or control or effectuating any political change . . . and doing any act . . . or
confederating together for the carrying out of said purposes.[71]

Thus, unless IWW members completely stopped meeting, talking, writing,
and helping others to organize, they could be summarily arrested and jailed.
This was a substantial obstacle to their political goal.

The precursor to this sort of injunction was one obtained against striking
workers at the Pullman Railroad Car Company in 1894. At the behest of the
Attorney General (a former employee of the Chicago Burlington and Quincy
Railroad), it forbade workers to interfere with, hinder, or stop "any of the
business of [certain listed railroads] or any . . . trains whether freight or pas-
senger." It also held anyone aiding or assisting such actions guilty as a
principle. The progeny of this original injunction grew to include not only
the one against the IWW, but over 70 percent of the injunctive cases in the
federal courts.[72]

These injunctions were not only broadly inclusive and exceedingly oppressive, but they were also *ex parte*. That is, they were issued without
the presence of the party enjoined in court. The idea behind *ex parte*
injunctions is that they will be quickly followed by hearings at which
everything will eventually be thrashed out. The *ex parte* injunction is
usually reasonable because there is an emergency and the hardship to the
enjoined party is less than that to the plaintiff. But in cases such as *IWW*
and *Pullman*, the injunctions were so broad and restrictive that they halted
the efficient circulation of discourse and the networking required to produce
power and to give it some directional effect. They sought to preserve the
established order by prohibiting any practices (verbal or physical) that did
not support it. They sought to kill the strike and the union, for which
they had some good reasons.

First, the criminal syndicalism with which the workers were often suspected was clearly a bad thing. People should not be allowed to aid or abet
crimes, sabotage, and all other manner of malicious mischief as a means of
accomplishing industrial or political change.[73] President Richard Nixon was
driven from office because of this type of activity, and many of his aides
received jail sentences for helping him. Second, the state governments faced
an interesting problem in that when they pursued convictions under criminal
syndicalism statutes—they were frustrated more often than not. Juries simply
found prosecution witnesses singularly unreliable.[74] Finally, you could be
convicted under those statutes for belonging to an organization which had

a goal that was arguably violative of the statute, even if you actively disagreed with that particular goal and worked assiduously to reorient the movement. Juries were not fond of this either (although sixty-year-old Anita Whitney was in fact convicted for exactly this and her conviction was upheld by the U.S. Supreme Court).[75]

So the attorneys general developed the idea of using the injunction in a different and more expeditious manner. As we said, unless IWW members completely stopped meeting, talking, writing, and aiding others to organize and become union members, they could be jailed before sufficient evidence to convict them of criminal syndicalism could come before a court. This would almost certainly halt all union activities, even those that were legal. If, for example, someone honestly did not believe that his or her behavior constituted criminal syndicalism and continued union activity, he or she could be summarily arrested and imprisoned for contempt; a result certainly giving pause to sympathizers and compatriots alike. Even if after months of testimony and appeal, he or she was vindicated, he or she had already been punished and the union quashed.

Injunctions, then, were powerful tools for the political enemies of labor early in this century and their use illuminates the exercise of this type of coercive power. Simply put, devising ways of punishing behavior that is seeking to change the ensemble of practices supporting a given order is itself a change in that ensemble of supporting practices. We might expect, then, that those devices could be turned around and used to support change. There are some interesting modern examples of this. One example comes from the mid–1960s, when state and local police throughout the South arrested civil rights leaders for subversion and seized their records under Communist control acts passed during the 1950s. This was a convenient way of making life burdensome and generally miserable for civil rights organizations. It also harassed the Supreme Court, which would ultimately have to overturn any such convictions based on statutes violative of the First Amendment as written or applied.

In response, the Southern Christian Education Fund (SCEF) began a revolution; a revolution of the same sort that the National Consumer's League had mustered with the Brandeis Brief. Concluding that discretion is the better part of valor in any confrontation between civil rights activists and local law enforcement officials, the SCEF sued to enjoin state officials from interfering with their efforts.[76] The resulting "Dombrowski-type Remedy" authorized federal courts to grant injunctive and declaratory relief against overly zealous official defenders of the *status quo*. The availability of the "Dombrowski-type Remedy," of course, "has the political effect of altering the balance of power between the citizen and the government, striking a more favorable balance between those who are trying to bring about social change and those who are seeking to resist it."[77] Like every politically legal device so far, the injunction has proven to be double edged.

PRIVATE JUDICIAL BODIES AND THE POLITICAL TRIAL

We have considered the major devices of our legal system and discovered each to be a viable political tool that has been and still is in constant and sometimes justifiable use for political purposes by all sorts of groups throughout our whole society. Of course, the available legal devices are by no means exhausted by the categories mentioned so far. Judges, for example, are empowered to issue contempt citations to punish unruly conduct in their courtrooms and chastise any outside activities that threaten the integrity of what goes on inside. This power is used to silence critics, punish counsel for unpopular causes, and dissuade members of the bar from taking controversial political cases.

A somewhat recent example is U.S. v. Dellinger, et al., a trial of eight well-known antiwar and civil rights activists charged with a conspiracy to cross state lines with the intent to start a riot at the 1968 Democratic convention.[78] Underlining his position as defender of "the federal system and state court legal system," Judge Julius Hoffman imposed contempt citations on attorneys and defendants alike so that everybody went to jail regardless of the trial's outcome.[79]

Similarly, after the "Battle of Foley Square," a 1949 Smith Act prosecution of Communist Party leaders, Judge Carlos Media announced forty contempt citations against the defense,[80] causing great consternation among Supreme Court justices, who nevertheless upheld the citations appeal.[81] An earlier example occurred in 1917 when the Supreme Court upheld the summary punishment of a Mister Quinlian, who, at a union meeting, criticized a local court's conduct of an ongoing trial, and the Toledo News Bee for publications critical of the Court's conduct in the Quinlian case.[82]

So the potential for turning a trial political runs not just broad but deep; a broad range of tools are available to the task, and once begun, a political trial can be made even more political through the inherent powers of the court. These include not just contempt citations but "gag orders," venue changes, rulings on the relevance of evidence, and decisions as to standing, jurisdiction, and ripeness. Each of these has been used, jointly or severally, in ways similar to the contempt citation.[83] But we should also be aware that political trials occur outside the formal public bodies focused on here, and that the private judicial bodies involved in those trials are often manipulated by government to exactly the good and bad ends we have been illustrating. This happens simply because power relationships are a web running throughout the whole society. They are interwoven with kinship relationships, family relationships, professional relationships, and social relationships, which they condition and by which they are themselves conditioned. Throughout this web, techniques are forever being sought in practice to allow power to circulate more efficiently, to close the gaps where resistance takes hold, and to disable the mechanisms through which counter moves might be taken.

A few brief examples should suffice. It is well known that prior to becoming president, John Adams successfully defended the British Captain Prescott against charges of ordering British troops to fire on colonists at the "Boston Massacre." This was a difficult thing for the future president to do primarily because of public opprobrium. This opprobrium echoed through the ages right down to the American Nazi Party, which had a difficult time finding counsel for the defense of their First Amendment rights when they wanted to march in a Jewish suburb of Chicago.[84] The habit of thus chilling a lawyer's duty is bad enough when engaged in by the public at large, but often it is encouraged and sustained through government activity.

Following the Second World War, public opprobrium was more than matched by the government during the Smith Act prosecutions of the Communist Party. In June 1946, Attorney General Tom Clark told the Chicago Bar Association that attorneys should be careful in their choice of clients and causes. In a popular magazine article printed during the prosecution of Communist Party members in New York's "Battle of Foley Square," he reiterated his concern with specific reference to attorneys serving Communist clients. Rising to the attorney general's challenge that recalcitrant lawyers be taken "to the legal woodshed for a definite and well-deserved admonition,"[85] the American Bar Association (ABA) recommended that bar associations throughout the country expel Communist Party members and advocates of Communist doctrines.

The local bars did better than that. They descended on the Foley Square defense counsel with an avidness that not even a direct rebuff by the Supreme Court could stem.[86] In consultation with the U.S. attorney general and the FBI, the New York Bar Association held its own hearings and then petitioned the federal courts to disbar both of the attorneys for the Communist Party leadership who were members of the New York Bar. The resulting disbarment order against one of the attorneys was eventually overturned, but the other was relentlessly pursued for over ten years before being dropped.

Of course, state and local actions of this sort multiplied. Often they were justified by reference to contempt citations issued to attorneys during trial for not answering questions from the bench about whether their past contained any Communist Party affiliation.[87] These actions eventually caused the ABA to pull itself together, reverse its policy, and rebuff the attorney general.[88] But the point was made that private organizations and their judicial bodies can become governmental instruments given the proper encouragement.

It should now be clear that political trials, although they are not always obvious, are everywhere. We can even say that they can be used to promote the ends of a plural democratic society as well as to hinder them and that often, to weed out the effects of bad political trials, we ought to cultivate good ones. So the question is not so much whether we will or should have political trials but what will count as political trials in different situations and what will at the same time count as their justification. What is the proper relationship between politics and law? Where, if anywhere, should we draw the line?

NOTES

1. C. H. Montange, "NEPA in an Era of Economic Deregulation: A Case Study of Environmental Avoidance at the Interstate Commerce Commission," 9 *Virginia Environmental Law Journal* 1–44, esp. 2–12 (Fall 1989).

2. E. McWhinney, *Supreme Courts & Judicial Law Making: Constitutional Tribunals & Constitutional Review* (Boston: Martinus NiJoff, 1986).

3. J. Grossman, et al., "Dimensions of Institutional Participation: Who Uses the Courts & How?" 44 *Journal of Politics* 86–114 (1982); H. Jacob, *Destiny in Court: The Consumption of Government Services* (Chicago, Rand McNally, 1969).

4. F. Zemans, "Legal Mobilization: The Neglected Role of the Law in the Political System," 77 *American Political Science Review* 690–703, note 6 (1983).

5. S. Daniels, "Civil Litigation in Illinois Trial Courts: An Exploration of Rural-Urban Differences," 4 *Law & Policy Quarterly* 190–214 (1984).

6. W. McIntosh, "Private Use of a Public Forum: A Long Range View of the Dispute Processing Role of Courts," 77 *American Political Science Review* 991–1010 (1983).

7. 250 U.S. 616 (1919).

8. H. Jacob, *Justice in America: Courts, Lawyers, and the Judicial Process* (Boston: Little, Brown and Co., 1978), 7.

9. C. H. Franklin and Diane C. Kosaki, "Republican School Master: The U.S. Supreme Court, Public Opinion & Abortion," 3 *American Political Science Review* 751–772 (September 1989).

10. N. Dorsen and L. Friedman, *Disorder in the Court* (New York: Pantheon Books, 1973), 81.

11. F. A. Allen, *The Crimes of Politics: Political Dimensions of Criminal Justice* (Cambridge: Harvard University Press, 1974), 53.

12. S. I. Kutler, *The American Inquisition: Justice and Injustice in the Cold War* (New York: Hill and Wang, 1982), 215–242.

13. See W. Gellhorn, ed., *The States and Subversion*, Chapter 7 (Ithaca: Cornell University Press, 1952), 358.

14. See *Debs v. U.S.*, 249 U.S. 211 (1919); *Goldman v. U.S.* 245 U.S. 474 (1919).

15. P. Renshaw, *The Wobblies: The Story of Syndicalism in the United States* (New York: Doubleday, 1968).

16. R. Dworkin, *Rebel in Paradise* (Chicago: University of Chicago Press, 1961).

17. R. J. Goldstein, "An American Gulag? Summary Arrest and Emergency Detention of Political Dissidents in the United States," 10 *Columbia Human Rights Law Review* 541–573 (1978).

18. N. Dorsen, et al., *Political and Civil Rights in the United States* (New York: Pantheon Books, 1976).

19. D. N. Hoffman, "Contempt of the United States: The Political Crime That Wasn't," 25 *The American Journal of Legal History* 343–360 (1981).

20. 64 Mass. 376 (1852).

21. Ibid., 377.
22. Ibid., 378.
23. Ibid., 380.
24. 59 N.C. 322 (1862).
25. Ibid.
26. *State v. Black*, 60 N.C. 262 (1864).
27. *State v. Rhodes*, 61 N.C. 453 (1868).
28. *State v. Mabry*, 64 N.C. 592 (1870).
29. 70 N.C. 60 (1874).
30. 444 U.S. 507 (1980).
31. Ibid., 508.
32. *Thornton and Wife v. Suffolk Manufacturing*, 64 Mass. 376 (1852), note 14; also see F. Meadows, "The First Amendment and the Secrecy State: *Snepp v. United States*," 130 *U. Pa. L.R.* 775 (1982); Comment, "*National Security and the First Amendment: The CIA and the Marketplace of Ideas*," 114 *Harv. L.R.* 665 (1983).
33. *U.S. v. Marchetti*, 466 F.2d 1309 (4th Cir., 1972).
34. *U.S. v. Snepp*, 456 F. Supp. 232 (1978).
35. *U.S. v. Snepp*, 595 F.2d 933 (1979).
36. See *Prepublication Review and Secrecy Requirements Imposed Upon Federal Employees: Hearings Before the Subcommittee on Civil and Constitutional Rights of the House Committee on the Judiciary*, 96th Cong., 2nd session, 19–20 (1981).
37. *Snepp v. U.S.*, 444 U.S. 509 (1979) note 3.
38. See Meadows, "The First Amendment and the Secrecy State," note 26.
39. *U.S. v. Crowthers*, 456 F.2d 1047 (4th Cir., 1972).
40. P. Agee, "Where Myth Leads to Murder," *Covert Action Information Bulletin*, July 1978, 6–7; also see his "Why I Split the CIA and Spilled the Beans," *Esquire*, June 1975, 128; and "A Spy in the Cold," *Newsweek*, Jan 28, 1980, 32.
41. See *New York Times*, March 21, 1977, 7, col. 1.
42. *Agee v. Vance*, 483 F. Supp. 729 (1980); *Agee v. Muskie*, 629 F.2d 80 (D.C. cir., 1980).
43. *Haig v. Agee*, 453 U.S. 308 (1981).
44. See *Frohwerk v. U.S.*, 249 U.S. 204 (1919).
45. Ibid., 209.
46. See R. Redish, "Advocacy of Unlawful Conduct and the First Amendment: In Defense of Clear and Present Danger," 70 *Calif. L.R.* 1159 (1982).
47. See *Frohwerk v. U.S.*, 249 U.S. 204 (1919); *Debs v. U.S.*, 249 U.S. 211 (1919); *Schneck v. U.S.*, 249 U.S. 48 (1919); *Dennis v. U.S.*, 341 U.S. 494 (1951); *U.S. v. O'Brien*, 391 U.S. 367 (1968).
48. See *Pierce v. U.S.*, 365 U.S. 292 (1966).
49. *Central Hudson Gas and Electric Corp. v. Public Service Commission*, 447 U.S. 557.
50. *Bigelow v. Virginia*, 421 U.S. 809 (1975).
51. 410 U.S. 113 (1973).
52. 635 P.2d 281 (1981); *cert. denied* 456 U.S. 929 (1982).
53. 489 F. Supp. 763 (N.D. Miss., 1980); *affirmed* 718 F.2d 738 (5th Cir., 1985); *cert. denied* 104 S.Ct. 3553 (1984).
54. *Roe v. Wade*, 410 U.S. 113 (1973).

55. See *Doe v. Commonwealth's Attorney For City of Richmond*, 425 U.S. 901 (1976); *Bowers v. Hardwick*, 478 U.S. 186 (1986).

56. *Bowers v. Hardwick*, 478 U.S. 186 (1986).

57. "Supplementary Detailed Staff Reports on Intelligence Activities and the Rights of Americans," Book III, *Final Report of the Select Committee to Study Governmental Operations with Respect to Intelligence Activities*, S. Rep. no. 94–755, 94th Cong. 2nd Sess. (1976), 551–552.

58. *Alien Enemies Act of 1798*, Ch. 6, 1 Stat. 577–8 (1798).

59. For a historical summary of this process see Goldstein, "An American Gulag?"

60. Ibid., 548–549, note 36.

61. Ibid., 544.

62. See C. Rossiter, *Constitutional Dictatorship* (Princeton, NJ: Princeton University Press, 1949), p. 227.

63. See W. Preston, *Aliens and Dissenters: Federal Suppression of Radicals 1903–1933* (New York: Harper and Row, 1969), 204–215.

64. Goldstein, "An American Gulag," 551.

65. S. Ungar, *FBI 43* (Boston: Little, Brown and Co., 1976), 48; M. Lowenthal, *The Federal Bureau of Investigation* (New York: Stoane Publishers, 1950), 289–300.

66. R. Goldstein, *Political Repression in Modern America: From 1870 to the Present*, 10 *Columbia Human Rights Law Review* 541 (1978).

67. Goldstein, "An American Gulag," 558–559.

68. Ibid., 562.

69. E. Brandeis, *The History of Labor in the United States, 1896–1932, Labor Legislation* (New York: Macmillan, 1935), volume 7.

70. See J. Goldmark, *Impatient Crusader, Florence Kelley's Life Story* (Urbana, IL: University of Illinois Press, 1953), 155–161.

71. See C. Marion, *The Communist Trial, An American Crossroads* (New York: Fairplay Publishers, 1953), 108.

72. See D. Novak, "The Pullman Strike Cases: Debs, Darrow, and the Labor Injunction," in M. R. Belknap, ed., *American Political Trials* (Westport, CT: Greenwood Press), 134–136.

73. This was the general import of the statutes in the thirty-three states that passed them, see *California General Laws* (Deering, 1934) Act 8428.

74. See A. Chaffee, *Free Speech in the United States* (Cambridge: Harvard University Press, 1967), 327.

75. *Whitney v. California*, 274 U.S. 357 (1927).

76. *Dombrowski v. Pfister*, 380 U.S. 479 (1965).

77. R. A. Sedler, "The Dombrowski-Type Suit as an Effective Weapon for Social Change: Reflections from Without and Within," 18 *Kansas L.R.* 237 (1970), p. 239.

78. No. 69 Crim. 180 (1969).

79. See M. Levine, *The Tales of Hoffman* (New York: Bantam Books, 1970), p. 260.

80. See S. Kutler, "Kill the Lawyers: Guilt by Representation," *The American Inquisition: Justice and Injustice in the Cold War* (New York: Hill and Wang, 1982), ch. 6.

81. Ibid., 159–164.

82. *Toledo Newspaper Co. v. U.S.*, 247 U.S. 402 (1917).

83. See *U.S. v. Berrigan*, 437 F.2d 750 (4th Cir. 1971).

84. See D. Goldberger, "The Right to Counsel in Political Cases: The Bar's Failure," 43 *Law and Contemporary Problems* 321 (1980).

85. Ibid.

86. Ibid., 165.

87. Ibid., 1.

88. See R. M. Belknap, *Cold War Political Justice* (Westport, CT: Greenwood Press, 1977), 223–231.

Chapter Two

Contrasting Theories of the Political Trial

Before we can use the courts to counter bad political trials, and before we can hope to use political trials to systematically promote plural democracy, we must understand what is meant by the term "political trial." The political trial has been used in a variety of ways in different intellectual traditions. It is employed directly and actively in major political struggles, particularly in underdeveloped nations and by groups struggling for the recognition of certain rights in the United States (e.g., the Gay Rights Movement, the Women's Movement). Consequently, it is used in different contexts, for different purposes, to make different points, and to describe and evaluate different situations and outcomes.[1]

Nevertheless, we can identify two broad and contrasting ideas of a political trial. The first holds that in most cases a political trial is clearly identifiable. There are certain necessary and sufficient conditions for the proper use of the term, and certain necessary evaluations follow from these conditions, which are generally negative. This approach to understanding political trials is usually taken by those arguing that no political consideration ever justifies bringing, prosecuting, or concluding a trial. The propriety of political trials is never in question. They are inherently unjustifiable, although they are perhaps inevitable and sometimes work out all right in the end. We will call this the "simple" idea of political trials.

The contrasting idea holds that the meaning of "political trial" is logically and practically problematic. There are degrees of "politicalness" to different trials and trials whose unquestionably political natures are overt or covert to different degrees. The nature of a trial at any given time depends on the ongoing social order. That order is constantly being restructured and is constantly redefining what counts as a political trial and what is politically necessary and justified as far as trials are concerned. Political trials occur (or do not occur) not because certain necessary or sufficient conditions are fulfilled (or not fulfilled), but because people share and engage in often recurring and regularly changing patterns or forms of interaction. These forms of interaction take on more or less political aspects and call for different kinds of political activity at different times and in different situations, some of which might reasonably involve the judiciary. It follows that political trials are more or less justified in different situations and, indeed, are a positive good at many points in the ongoing course of events. This being the case, it is a question of what sort of circumstances make a trial political and what sort of circumstances justify political trials. We will call this the "complex" idea of a political trial.

Under the complex idea, we can further divide the political trial into two different types: The negative type in which courts are used to bother people for political purposes in ways they should not, and the positive type in which courts bother people for political purposes in ways they should. Our civilization's values and its approach to the problem of the permissible limits of coercion depends on how it answers the questions of when, to what extent, for what purposes, and in relation to what courts ought to interfere with people to realize political ends.

Which of these ideas is correct? Our argument that political trials can be justified and used to positive ends clearly requires that the complex idea be accepted. But it is not obviously correct. Even the brief history sketched in chapter 1 reveals good reasons for adopting the simple idea and its negative attitude. Briefly, those holding to the simple idea correctly perceive that independent courts are the best way to constrain our political institutions so as to ensure that ours is a government under law and not subject to the individual biases of well-intentioned individuals. Once a fusion of judicial and legislative or executive functions occurs, the courts cross the line into political action and the calculus of their reasoning is biased by the particular political, social, or economic goals and values they are promoting at the moment. Not only do the courts abdicate the functions of preserving and protecting more profound values and guarding against official overreach, they make things worse by actually engaging in the behavior they are meant to constrain. Some Pyrrhic victories for what is currently perceived as "just" are thus purchased at the price of long-term losses of the most fundamental kind.

Those holding to the simple idea perceive another evil as well. Courts are meant to apply laws embodying goals and values thrashed out by the people and articulated through their elected representatives in the executive and legislative branches. Courts that make rather than implement values and goals are in effect subverting the system.

In the following sections, we will show why the simple idea is inadequate even to meet the problems of fusion they identify. We will also develop the complex idea in its negative and positive senses and consider its implications in light of when and for what ends political trials might be justified. Finally, we will identify the types of political trials that can best redress whatever imbalances of social and political power come to be reflected in our courts.

FUNDAMENTAL PROBLEMS WITH THE SIMPLE IDEA

The simple idea of political trials would be correct if law and politics could be kept distinct. While we have seen that in practice there is a fusion of functions between the obviously political branches and the courts, it may be that this fusion occurs simply because our flesh is weak. That is, it just might be that we ought to keep the functions of each branch separate. But if we cannot keep the two apart, if politics and law cannot be delimited, there must be a good reason and the complex idea would be more correct. Since it is human beings that fuse and separate according to their intentions, we must understand what is meant by the terms "politics" and "law" in order to justify the complex view.

The Nature of Politics and Law

Historically, three general ideas have persevered about the nature of law. The first is the natural theory of law, which emphasizes the relationship between law and morality. It sees the origin and justification of law in either "right reason" or revelation and is the only theory to ever really suggest that law and politics might be distinct. It embraces the concept of a "higher law" as a check on the general social, political, and economic scramble.

The second idea is the positive theory of law. It emphasizes the relationship between law and political power, and it understands human political institutions to be the sole source and measure of the law. This idea fuses law and politics absolutely. Law is simply one way of exercising political power.

The third idea is the sociological theory, and it emphasizes the relationship between law and the historical development of a community's social structure. It sees the source and the justification of law in the sometimes consensual, sometimes conflicting social interactions of groups and individuals. Here, law and politics are distinct but interdependent. Each implies the other. There can be no law without society, and at some point in its development, society requires law. The social interaction that produces law is politics, and the law in turn has social and political effects.[2]

We intend to demonstrate that a close analysis of the natural and positivist views leads us to an acceptance of the sociological view. This conclusion, in turn, requires that we abandon the idea that the proper relationship between politics and law can be anything but problematic, protean, and permutable and leads us to accept the idea that political trials must sometimes occur and must therefore, sometimes be good. Finally we hope to demonstrate the most important conclusion: The sociological theory and the complex idea of law provide the means for determining when a trial is political and when a political trial is good.

We begin by first stating that the natural and positivist approaches stress the importance of rules and coercive power in politics and law. Thomas Aquinas says, for example, that "a law is imposed on others as a rule and measure," and "Law is nothing else but a dictate of practical reason emanating from the ruler."[3] His idea is simply that there exists a transcendent law that can be known (indeed, *must* be known) and must be enforced by temporal rulers as a positive obligation. Similarly, Thomas Hobbes is sure that "civil law is to every subject, those rules, which the commonwealth hath commanded him, by . . . sufficient sign of will, to make use of, for the distinction of . . . what is contrary, and what is not contrary to the rule."[4] Parallel characterizations can be found in the writings of J. Austin, H.L.A. Hart, and H. Kelson.[5]

So the rules, whether from God or the chief executive, come from on high in any case, and power puts the rules into practice as laws. For those who accept the natural law approach, law and politics are distinct because the politics involved are merely a conduit for something discovered or revealed in another context (e.g., the church, the laboratory, a class in secular humanism). For people who accept the positive law approach, law and politics are fused because law is merely a symptom of the "politicking" of those in power.

Certain problems, however, crop up with both of these ideas about rules (laws) and power (politics). "Rules," "knowing rules," "power," and "having power" are meaningless unless understood from a sociological point of view because what counts as "knowing" and "having" is a result of social practice and agreement. At first, this may seem like a strange statement, but it is not arbitrary and is the result of much thought and self-criticism. If we are right, this idea solves many problems concerning political trials and their justification, as we will demonstrate in later chapters.

Rules

First, let's consider rules. One bothersome thing about them is that it is impossible for any set of them to completely determine their own application.[6] "However many rules you give me, I [must] give a rule which justifies *my* employment of your rules."[7] This is simply the problem of infinite regress. One needs rules to justify the employment of rules. Yet, on a day-to-day basis, we end this regression in some manner that does not seem arbitrary to us. Both the natural and positivist approaches attempt to resolve this difficulty by pointing to an arbitrary end point postulated as the ultimate source of the rules (e.g., God, the innate properties of matter, those in power). But the attempt is unsuccessful. We can always ask, Why obey God?

Why obey those in power? Why not overcome or control nature (the innate properties of matter)? These questions lead us back to the infinite regress of rules (e.g., "Obey those who can hurt you." "Why?" "Don't experience pain." "Why?").

Faced with this situation, the best we can do to justify or explain our behavior is to say, "This is simply what I do." Now this is not acting arbitrarily; rather, it means that "following a rule" or "knowing a rule" is a custom, practice, or institution. It presupposes a society. If the practices, customs, and institutions disappear, so do rules. Consider, for example, this annotated version of Wittgenstein's famous rumination:

How does it come about that this arrow *points* [i.e., is a kind of rule telling us where to go]? Doesn't it seem to carry in it something beside itself [i.e., "higher law"]? . . . [No,] the arrow points only in the application that a living being makes of it. It is custom and practice that both constitute "following the rule" and "knowing" or "understanding" the rule of this arrow [e.g., "go that way"]; and even though the arrow seems to embody something more compelling, that is just an artifact of how we learned that the arrow points [i.e., tacitly, through social practice].[8]

Pointing is not a property of the arrow itself, suggesting something above or beyond social practice and the arrow that informs our understanding. And it is custom or the practices of proceeding that constitute following and "knowing" legal rules as well.

Similarly, "knowing a rule" does not necessarily begin with a particular formulation about how to act. When we count, we usually do not begin by saying, "All right, the rule is n, n + 1, n + 2, n + 3." Rather, we say, "One, two, three." The formal rule may never occur to us. There may be no point to formalizing the practice in a statement about how to proceed. Yet, don't we "know a rule" by knowing how to proceed? After doing it for a while we might say, "Ah! This can be formalized," but did we know a rule before making this statement?

The point is that "knowing a rule" and "following a rule" do not require pre-existing formal statements or even any particular state of consciousness. They are practices. When a judge says, "We have done *this* in this case, and *this* in another case, and then *this* in a third, hence we must do this now because there is the following rule," it does not mean that the rule is only just being created. The judge is, rather, reminding us of our practice (or perhaps articulating our practice as a formal statement for the first time) and, in so doing, pointing at actions that are the rule. The claim that some rules do not exist before the instance in which they find formalization is, therefore, inaccurate. If there is only one instance of practice to look at, that is the rule. The single case "points" (as does the arrow) according to the use made of it by the judge at that time. If, on the other hand, we can find no case (no practice) on the specific issue at hand, we look at our principles (e.g., as laid out in the Constitution) and our social, political, and economic policies to remind us of how we practice generally.[9] These provide the model or paradigm (albeit a very general one) for dealing with the issue.

The central point is that the concepts of "knowing a rule" and "following a rule" and consequently "rules" themselves result from the characteristics and recurrent practices of a society as a whole. A rule coming from above, from outside those practices, could not be understood. It would be historically and culturally meaningless, although some meaning derived from social practice and history would probably be projected on the rule by the population at large especially if some need was perceived for doing so (e.g., if they were the edict of a foreign conqueror or they had the imprimatur of God or the Church). But whatever meaning it might possibly have would necessarily grow out of interpersonal relationships, customs, and traditions developed in response to technological changes and changes in social organization.

Through this investigation of the logic of the natural and positivist views, we come to an acceptance of the sociological view. The meaning of rules of law and even what counts as a law must come from the bottom up as well as from the top down. Law is in this sense an agreement, compromise, or balance worked out through sometimes conflictual, sometimes consensual, social interaction.

Power

Examining the logic of the natural and positivist view of power can also lead us to a sociological way of thinking. Power, as we already mentioned, is the key ingredient in natural and positive approaches to realizing the rules in practice. Power must be possessed by one person or group and exercised over another. But actually, power is reciprocal; it is a relationship, and it requires a group dynamic. Given the way power is generally used (e.g., Hobbes and Machiavelli) it is neither logically nor sociologically possible for an individual to be powerful alone. Consequently, a second person is required over whom to exercise power, which suggests that in even the most brutal instances of subordination there is a considerable degree of choice that might be exercised by the oppressed.[10] Its exercise, of course, involves sacrifices that we would usually never think of making. But a subordinate's freedom is never really destroyed totally, short of destroying the subordinate. At that point, however, the superior's power over the subordinate is lost as well. One does not have power over a dead person.

But if power is reciprocal, can a subordinate exercise power over a superior? It does seem that the master might be the slave of the slaves. To benefit from the exercise of power, the superior must convince the subordinate to yield. Consequently, short of constant physical coercion, the superior must make yielding desirable. The subordinate, therefore, has power over how the superior realizes the benefits of exercising power. There are, therefore, some things the superior simply cannot do and expect a return. Consequently, the subordinate, to some extent, determines the behavior of the superior.

Something, however, does not ring true with this scenario. In everyday experience we find this reciprocity but it does not seem to provide a check on the use of power. Something that seems to have objective determinants allows us to say "because of this, this person, finally, has power." How is this possible?

To begin with, power is not an objective entity that can be passed about. It is a highly complex social interaction embedded in meaningful contexts in which certain objective factors have meaning. No factors by themselves, abstracted from one or more concrete situations, determine where power will reside. Pure determinants of power are necessarily derivative. Keeping this in mind, we can say that one person has power because we are engaged in certain practices or ways of living together that are not the result of the exercise of power. When we make a theoretical investigation, we do not find ultimate factors that determine who has power, but an ultimate practice, a "form of life." We act in certain ways in certain contexts, not because we must, but because we just do it that way.

On this point, Wittgenstein says, "If I have exhausted the justifications I have reached bedrock, and the spade is turned. Then I am inclined to say, 'this is simply what I do.' " Similarly, just as "to obey a rule, to make a report, to play a game of chess, are *customs*,[11] so the exercise of power is simply a way we do things. Doing it that way has meaning in terms of our values and cultural history and is intelligible in terms of the struggles, strategies, tactics, and practices we develop to solve our problems within that larger context. If we want to engage in meaningful human interaction at all, one party must at some point accede, and that point is context dependent and socially learned. Accession, of course, is not logically (abstractly) necessary, but humanly (socially) necessary. "It is not true that it *must*—but it *does* follow and we *perform* this transition."[12]

Consider, for example, Kamikaze pilots. In what sense can we say that they engaged in meaningful behavior? Within the patterns, institutions, and customs of the Allied forces against whom they fought, their missions were suicidal, meaningless gestures. For the Allies, the point had been reached at which their customs and learned patterns of behavior in power relationships called for the accession of the Japanese pilots. One fought to the utmost and paid any price until the point was reached at which there was no possibility of winning. Then one acceded and hoped for the best in working out an armistice, became a prisoner of war and tried to escape, or ran away to return and fight another day. But to keep on fighting in a way that ensured your demise was meaningless. The pilots did not *logically* have to surrender, but they had to surrender to behave in a way meaningful to the Allies.

The Japanese had quite a different view. Acts such as these had meaning within their social practices or forms of life. Their customs, institutions, and practices extolled the virtues of such behavior. It was glorious and spiritually meaningful to die at such moments, to embrace death as actively as one embraced life, to end at the peak of one's capacity in one brilliant, selfless flame. So no factor or set of factors was agreed upon and shared between the Allies and the Japanese that might have served as objective determinants of the power relationship in Kamikaze situations. Two different views of what was meaningful under the same set of circumstances, two different models of the world learned and understood as social practice, implied two different ideas of what was too high a price to pay (or even what counted as paying any price at all) and resulted in what was meaningless behavior to one side of the struggle.

Once again, if we follow the meaning of power to its logical conclusion, which is so important to the natural and positivist schools, we come to an acceptance of the sociological school. That is, power, like following a rule or knowing a rule, grows out of interpersonal relationships—customs and traditions developed in response to many technical and cultural factors affecting social organizations. Exactly what power is and who has it and to what extent are products of social learning, practice, and evolution.

This analysis has important implications for the relationship between politics and law and, thus, for the controversy between the simple and complex ideas and evaluations of political trials. If we are to talk meaningfully about power and rules, politics and law, we must begin with the sociological view of the nature of law and this implies the complex idea of political trials because of the following:

1. Power is coextensive with the social body

2. Power relationships are interwoven with, condition, and are conditioned by other relationships

3. These relationships involve much more than prohibition and punishment

4. Law, legal discourse, and the institutions that produce them are part of the political economy of truth in our society (i.e., part of the ordered procedures for the production, distribution, circulation, and regulation of statements about whom power shall serve in these relationships and how it shall operate)

5. The law and its trials are always available as tools to make possible different modes of political and economic management at all levels of society and with regard to all of the relationships with which power is interwoven.

Situational considerations of the historical practices, social organizations, traditions, and understandings of the people involved are essential to determine whether we have political trials. Contrary to what the simple idea of political trial implies, what serves as a political trial is problematic and not predetermined. It is a result of human judgment in the context of ongoing forms of life and changing understandings.

Criteria for Evaluating Political Trials

At this point, we have left ourselves open to a serious charge. It might seem that we are retreating into radical subjectivism. If a political trial is really so protean, we can never really be sure that any trial is actually political or what its being political actually means. We are adrift; all of our subjective evaluations of trials as political or nonpolitical, good or bad, are equally valid and equally useless as guides to social action.

Actually, this objection misunderstands what it means to "know" something, as we explained earlier in discussing what it means to "know a rule." But we can best answer this charge by summarizing what we have just gone through in a slightly different way. Specifically, political trials have objective criteria notwithstanding everything we have just said. Those criteria, however, are learned from a variety of contexts, change historically, and may occur in a nearly infinite number of different combinations. Additionally, the contexts themselves are part of the objective meaning. They are subtle occasions for the proper use of "political trial," should some combination of certain other criteria be present.

Of course, the learning and changing of contexts and criteria is often the result of an agreement among the members of some relevant group—an agreement on conventions and a conceptual network that pulls the world together in a way that works. Such conventions are neither arbitrary in the sense that they could be just any other way, nor so malleable that they might be changed in any other way according to our whim. The situations in which people live have a natural and a cultural history, both of which restrict the kinds of negotiated agreements we can make. Certain agreements that we might imagine may simply be physically impossible. Others are historically or culturally impossible. For a form of life to exist, continuity must exist; there must be a shared history of human behavior. It is not that we could not go beyond or act outside our culture or history, but such activity would be socially irrelevant or historically meaningless.

Many people will find this response to the charge of subjectivism unsatisfactory. After all, we seem to be stressing the importance of the individual case in understanding when there is a political trial, and at the same time, we are insisting that individual cases cannot be all that unique if they are to be understood. If what counts as a political trial is to depend on some general understandings, then some common features are indispensable. We insist, however, that it is not the case that the common features *are* the political trials, nor that there must be a political trial where any particular common features exist. We also deny that the meaning of political trial (even in specific situations) is identical with or derivable from the common features. We will only say that where there are political trials there must be common features across time and among instances. Apparently, we are trying to have the best of both worlds—the advantages of the simple and complex conceptualizations. How can we do this?

The answer lies in the idea of "family resemblances."[13] If we consider a group of people, it may become obvious at some point that they all belong to the same family even though none share any particular set of features. Indeed no two members of the group need have any feature in common for all the members to be immediately recognizable as part of the same family. Bodies do not divide neatly into separate features, and even if we could isolate features easily, there are infinite gradations of "square chins" or "aquiline noses."

So it is with political trials. They share characteristics in infinite gradation. We learn, through experience, practice, and socialization, what is too divergent or unfamiliar to be included. In other words, it is true that there are objective justifications for the proper use of "political trial" and that political trials have little in common except that we agree to designate them as such. But in any case, we have the best of both worlds. We have shared characteristics, but each trial is unique.

If recognizing what counts as a sufficient resemblance to call a trial political is the result of social practice, how can anyone from outside the society or culture recognize a political trial in that society? Won't any analysis we give be culture bound? Well, this is a little bit right and a little bit wrong. For many political trials, outside investigators will have to familiarize themselves with the society they are studying before they can confidently categorize the trials as good or bad. However, there will be cases in which the meaning of "political trial" is clear to those not participating in the relevant form of life but only observing from the sidelines. This is because we all participate in a human form of life beyond the array of conventions arranged by particular cultures because of their history and according to their convenience. These conventions are fixed neither by custom nor by agreement, but rather by the nature of human life itself. All language use and all conceptualization within a language takes place within these necessarily shared human conditions. Without these regularities "which no one has doubted, but which have escaped remark only because they are always before our eyes,"[14] no basis for understanding exists. It is their participation in the human form of life that enables objective observers to look at the right things for an understanding of political trial in a culture other than their own.

So far, two contrasting conceptualizations of political trial and three theories about the nature of law have been examined. The natural and positivist theories have been shown to lead us, in the course of their logic, to an acceptance of the sociological theory as the more correct view, and this has led to an understanding that the simple idea of political trial is most probably mistaken. In short, whether or not a trial is political and the degree of its politicalness must be determined on a case-by-case basis according to the purposes, history, and sociology of the people involved and the people asking the question.

But up to this point the discussion has been entirely too abstract, especially regarding how we might have objective criteria without benefit of necessary and sufficient conditions. We must now substantiate our claims by concrete examples of the simple idea of political trial, how the complex idea improves thereon, and exactly how our culturally and historically developed agreements as to the meaning and evaluation of political trial save us from subjectivism and allow social action to redress the imbalance of power in our society through good political trials.

Defining Political Trials

Perhaps the most direct of the simple approaches to defining political trials is that of T. I. Becker in his "Introduction" to *Political Trials*. The distinguishing characteristics of a political trial are taken to be the "calculated use of the court-forum by any party to a political struggle" caused by a "perception of a direct threat to (that party's) political power"[15] in order to eliminate either "pesky irritants or deadly challenges."[16] Given that definition, there are four kinds of political trials:

(1) political trials, referring to situations in which defendants have purposively ignored or flaunted existing laws in order to bring about drastic social change

(2) political "trials," referring to a situation in which the impartiality and independence of the court is questionable

(3) "political" trials, wherein the court may be independent and impartial but the political motivation for bringing the suit is hidden

(4) "political trials," combining the worst aspects of "political" trials and political "trials."[17]

Normally, the first type of political trial is not bad. Individuals challenging the system in this way "are enemies of whichever system happens to be legally established at the time, and they are all adjudged accordingly."[18] But the other three types of political trials are bad. "What actually rankles people about political trials are the connotations of deception or unfairness"[19] attaching to each of the other three. Of course, these evaluations follow naturally from the definition of political trial; they are the working out of the various permutations and implications of its meaning.

Now, we must be suspicious of this approach. First of all, a significant problem in analytical thinking revolves about the fact that often "you have a new concept and interpret it as seeing a new object. You interpret a grammatical movement made by yourself as a Quasi-physical phenomenon which you are observing."[20] In Becker's case, because of the tightly logical nature of his model, it is possible that certain of his conclusions and evaluations may be founded on "grammatical movements" within his model. That is, his perceptions of the types of political trials possible and his normative insights may be, to some significant extent, creations of the language of his model. They may be tendencies more of the particular logic of his model's grammar than the physical world to which it is meant to refer. By impressing this particular model on the phenomena he is observing, Becker seems to fix the sense or meaning of political trial. But we must notice that the actual uses of the term are much muddier than he allows, as can be seen from the examples given in the first chapter. Narrowing the concept in the way he does may ignore many forms of political trial whose impact is significant on human affairs. It may also bias our evaluation of political trials in certain ways.

In light of Becker's evaluations, let's consider the question of whether or not trials of individuals who have purposely violated certain laws in order to bring about social change are bad. Becker, of course, does not argue that such trials are good. They are simply not bad. They are part of "a natural cycle in many political dramas."[21] This neutral evaluation must follow from his definition of political trial. For if political trial is defined as the calculated use of courts by any party to a political struggle, that must include those with whom we agree as well as those with whom we disagree. To avoid an obvious bias, political trials of this type must be considered normatively neutral.

We notice, first of all, that not every use of the court-forum to eliminate pesky irritants or deadly challenges is called a political trial. When people bring suit against the FBI, the CIA, the local police, or the local district attorney for illegally tampering with their mail, invading their bedrooms without a warrant, illegally tapping their phone, for police brutality, or for false arrest, we do not call it a political trial. We usually consider it an affirmation of our constitutional rights (a pursuit of law, not politics), even though those bringing suit may be pursuing political change (Martin Luther King, Jr.), economic change (Ralph Nader), or social change (Bobby Seal, Eldridge Cleaver). Nor would we consider the bringing of such suits to be morally neutral. Most would consider them positive goods (perhaps even to the point of constituting a social duty), necessary for strengthening and maintaining the checks and balances in our society against the abuse of governmental power. While we could call these political trials (and evaluate them accordingly), in fact, we do not in our ordinary discourse. We do not because within our form of life, within the interpersonal relationships, customs, traditions, institutional arrangements, and day-to-day interactions that have historically developed among us, we do not consider them as such. To call trials in which individuals assert such constitutional rights political and morally neutral is, therefore, nonsensical in our day-to-day discourse and to those involved in the legal process. It seems, then, that Becker's rigorous application of a formal set of necessary and sufficient conditions for the use of political trials has misled us in two ways: first, regarding what is and is not a political trial (i.e., our social reality) and, second, regarding how that reality is evaluated.

Let's consider another example. Under Becker's definition, trials for acts of civil disobediences are political trials. Civil disobedience is a clear challenge to established political power, and the court forum is calculated by at least one of the parties (and often both) to be a means of eliminating the irritation or deadly challenge of the other. Once again, Becker would evaluate a normal trial of those engaging in acts of civil disobedience as morally neutral—part of the "natural cycle" of "political drama."

Our day-to-day discourse on civil disobedience, however, is not so clear as all this. Many would not call the trial of such dissidents political. Rather, it would be legal so long as they clearly violated some established law and the trial was normally conducted. To many others, however, it would be clearly political. Regardless of what laws were on the books, many view civil disobedience as an act addressed to those in power, guided by and directed at preserving the Constitution and our political institutions from what they perceive to be a threat from those holding positions of authority. As Rawls indicates:

Civil disobedience ... is one of the stabilizing devices of a constitutional system, although by definition, an illegal one ... by resisting injustice within the limits of fidelity to law, it serves to inhibit departures from justice and to correct them when they occur.[22]

In short, we do not all agree on the definition of disobedience. Consequently, we do not agree on the "politicalness" of its trial, or whether such trials are good or bad. If, for example, civil disobedience is honestly engaged in to secure a just end once reasonable options have been exhausted, it would seem to be a legitimate and perhaps necessary form of political participation (consider Thoreau and Gandhi). As such, it would not be a morally neutral act, but a good act from the standpoint of certain prevalent understandings of what constitutes justice and democracy. Others, of course, would disagree. They would argue that civil disobedience threatens the ultimate integrity of the state, necessarily leading (to some extent at least) to a breakdown of legitimate authority. Consequently, the ability of political institutions to effectively and fairly respond to and deal with situations and circumstances causing civil disobedience would be weakened as well.

Because of our history, customs, traditions, and social orientation, we are ambivalent about whether trials for civil disobedience are political trials, and about whether they are good or bad. Moreover, such judgments differ with context and time. Different individuals and groups look at the same behavior and recognize different elements of the situation as the paramount, the only important, or the most significant elements. They value different behaviors (e.g., dissent versus obedience, direct participation versus following proper channels through political representatives) and have different priorities. They recognize that they must work to maintain their view against the rival and that perhaps no resolution is possible through argument alone. We see no need as a society to choose one set of values and priorities over another in this case because we hold both sets of values and priorities simultaneously. Each simply comes to the fore in different contexts and for different purposes. Some optimum complex interrelationship of values and priorities is thus worked out through the practice of a sustained and continuous competition. This is part of our form of life, and the necessary and sufficient conditions for a political trial that are blocked out by Becker simply mislead and distort our understanding of what serves as a political trial.

An effect that our form of life has on our understanding and evaluation of political trials is evident in N. Dorsen's and L. Friedman's *Disorder in the Court*.[23] Distinctions are made therein among "politically motivated trials" (trials instigated by in groups to promote obvious political ends), "politically determined trials" (trials whose outcomes are affected by the political attitudes and considerations of the participants but which are not politically motivated),[24] and "political agitation in the courtroom" (a calculated use by a defendant of the court-forum to convey a political message to the widest possible audience).[25]

Dorsen and Friedman recognize something of the wider scope of uses for political trials that we find in our day-to-day discourse. But they have abstracted from our still more variable uses only those carrying implicit negative evaluations. Moreover, there is a tacit assumption that law and politics are distinct and that should they merge the result would necessarily be bad. This may be because most of the experts they use for substantiation are lawyers, judges, or professors of law who would understandably stress the independence of their discipline (e.g., radical defense counselor, William Kunstler, civil liberties lawyer Malcolm Bernstein, Columbia law professor Richard Uviller).[26] We might say, then, that Dorsen and Friedman have developed their "perspicuous overview" from a biased sample and thus produced a biased evaluation.

This tendency to abstract only the negative aspects of our day-to-day uses of political trials is perhaps most obvious in Dorsen and Friedman's use of Otto Kirchheimer's near-definitive work *Political Justice: The Use of Legal Procedure for Political Ends*.[27] In this work, "political trial" undergoes an evolution. Beginning with the "simplest and crudest" idea that "the courts eliminate a political foe of the regime according to some prearranged rules,"[28] it quickly passes on to a more sophisticated set of categories, only one of which (the "Classical political trial") fits the simplest definition.[29] Kirchheimer culminates this process with the idea that "in a political trial . . . the judicial machinery and its trial mechanics are set in motion . . . to exert influence on the distribution of political power."[30] This can clearly include good and bad uses of the judicial machinery; an influence that might, for example, redistribute political power in a more equitable manner (e.g., enforcing the Voting Rights Act).

But Dorsen and Friedman pick out of this process the definition of only one type of political trial that Kirchheimer uses to develop his definition. Their chosen definition is "governments and private groups (try) to enlist the support of the courts for upholding or shifting the balance of political power."[31] This formulation is not too different than the final formulation, but the differences are important when it comes to evaluating political trials. The differences are as follows:

1. In this definition, government and private groups enlist court support, while in the final definition, the "judicial machinery" is "set in motion."
2. The point of a political trial in this definition is to "uphold or shift the balance of political power," while in the final definition, the point is to "exert an influence on the distribution of political power."

There is an implication in the definition that Dorsen and Friedman use that some private group or the government is making a grab for power. They are not just asserting their rights in order to redress a moderate imbalance that has developed in practice or trying to more equally distribute power— possibilities that arise under Kirchheimer's final definition. They are definitely "shifting the balance." Someone gets what someone else loses, and the clear implication is that either government or some private group benefits rather than the public at large. Kirchheimer's final definition, on the other hand, clearly encompasses the possibility that influence might be exerted on behalf of the public. Dorsen and Friedman thus bias the evaluation of political trials by their choice of definition.

It seems as if Otto Kirchheimer's definition of political trial is the best. It certainly provides the broadest category of uses so far. Still, the definition is unsatisfying. It does not allow for all the uses in even the short list provided in the opening chapter. Similarly, in stressing the characteristic of using courts to influence the political flow of power, Kirchheimer's definition ignores such political uses of trials as those meant to dramatize the reality of the community and reinforce the sense of identity of community members.[32]

The problem is that Kirchheimer, like the others considered so far, conceptualizes the function of the political trial as representing the world to us; to depict or describe a possible state of affairs. "Political trial" is like a picture in the way it corresponds to things in the world. This picture might be accurate or inaccurate depending upon how well it agrees with reality—how well are the necessary and sufficient conditions for its use distinguishable in the situation it is meant to represent? According to this view, understanding a concept means knowing "the situation that is represented,"[33] what would count as verification and falsification, and "what is the case if it is true."[34] "Political trial," then, has only one correct, complete analysis.

But this cannot be the case. Words can be used as labels for states of affairs, but they are not always used that way, and some (e.g., "whether," "the," "when," "interlude") are never so used. Meanings of words are built up, generated, and changed, extended, and restricted by their use in various cases. Consequently, we cannot meaningfully speak of necessary and sufficient conditions for their use:

> Consider for example the proceedings that we call "games." I mean board-games, card-games, ball-games, Olympic games, and so on. What is common to them all? Don't say: "There must be something common, or they would not be called 'games' "—but look and see whether there is anything common at all—for if you look at them you will not see something that is common to all, but similarities, relationships, and a whole series of them at that. To repeat: don't think, but look! And the result of this examination is: we see a complicated network of similarities overlapping and crisscrossing: sometimes overall similarities, sometimes similarities of detail. I can think of no better expression to characterize these similarities than "family resemblances;" for the various resemblances between members of a family: build, features, color of eyes, gait, temperament, etc., overlap and crisscross in the same way. And I shall say: "games" form a family.[35]

What is being argued here is that a political trial is different in different times and places. Its proper use is not restricted in any way by factors outside the history, needs, understandings, and purposes of the people using the term. It is not that the term "political trial" is meaningless in the last analysis or that the definitions offered so far are wrong. Rather, they are not, and cannot be, complete. What they do indicate is that we must gain a still more perspicuous overview of its uses than that provided by Becker, Dorsen and Friedman, and Kirchheimer.

There is some movement toward a more perspicuous overview in the literature on political crimes. F. A. Allen has argued that "the definition of a political crime is itself a political question"[36] and that "the actual definitions accepted in various countries . . . have proved fluid and more often than not, have reflected political conditions."[37] What serves as a political trial, then, is context dependent; it depends to some extent on the objective (but changing) political forces involved. Additionally, Allen explains the difficulty average Americans have in accepting the idea of political trial, since "the American republic has not experienced a bloody revolution which pitted class against class, it has not been oppressed by an autocratic or totalitarian government, and it has not suffered the rule of a foreign conqueror or of a puppet regime installed by a foreign conqueror."[38] Furthermore, "the very diversity of pluralism has led many to believe that they are not doomed to occupy a minority position on all important issues."[39] In other words, the history, customs, traditions, and general form of life of American society makes it difficult for average Americans to conceive of political trials. Few trials appear to be political trials to most Americans.

On the other hand, Allen argues that recently the American concept of political trial is beginning to develop. This development is the result of a crisis in the American form of life that renders custom, tradition, and history less certain guides than they have been in the past:

The reality seeking expression in the language of "political prisoner" cannot be safely dismissed as part of a common-sense rejection of the vocabulary employed. One measure of the seriousness of the present crisis is the demonstrated incapacity of common sense—of the conventional wisdom—to supply an adequate understanding of the problems faced or to suggest means through which wise responses can be made. The common sense of the community may prove sufficient when it arises out of a community of experiences and circumstances, which in turn give life to widely shared views about behavior and events. Unfortunately, the most pressing and difficult issues have emerged precisely in those areas in which this commonality of experience, and hence of understanding and outlook, are lacking. In these matters, the common sense of the suburb is not the common sense of the ghetto. Nor, because each has in some sense lived in a different world, is the common sense of the old identical with that of the young.[40]

Thus, average Americans, because of changes in their form of life are experiencing changes in their ideas, including ideas about what serves as a political trial.

The danger, of course, is that things may go too far. While it is important to recognize the polymorphic nature of political trials (i.e., that there is no right situation for its use), it is also important intellectually, socially, and politically to recognize that there are right and wrong situations for its use. It is important intellectually because this same analysis can be applied to any concept, and if we cannot devise a way of distinguishing right and wrong uses of terms we cannot talk meaningfully about anything. Thus, not only is it meaningless to talk of "political trials" but to talk of "good" and "bad" as well. It is important socially and politically because such an understanding certainly includes the fundamentals of social organization. For some time now, psychoanalysts have appreciated the fact that people are hungry for sustaining political ideologies.[41] This apparently arises from two fundamental needs: (1) to feel secure and effective, people need a way to get their normative and objective bearings in the complex, highly mobile, rapidly changing societies of today; and (2) there is a fundamental human need to be part of a transcendental, transpersonal, common movement or purpose that will survive beyond the individual and give meaning to existence.[42]

Law, as expressed through the institution of our courts has always been a traditional source of these orientations and a means of securing this identification. The attractiveness of the simple approach is that when in the courts, politics and law must act within well-defined spheres to protect and promote specific values. The dedication to rational or revealed truth and the conclusion that right and wrong, good and bad, can be unreservedly identified helps to create and objectify an integrated social reality that we can all understand as good and satisfying, at least with regards to the two basic needs just identified. For this reason, it is important that our law maintain some rational integrity and that it employ reason to justify its activity. Our social, economic, and political history has simply brought us to the point where we identify the good with reason, and this identification ultimately sustains our society.

The simple fact is that we must provide some way of employing our reason to determine what constitutes a political trial and which political trials are good so that we can maintain the integrity of our courts as institutions reflecting, embodying, and promoting the application of reason to human affairs. Thus, we must now demonstrate a method through which we can analyze specific situations in concrete terms to determine which situations are political trials and which are not. For this we must look to the characteristic uses of political trial in our society, gain a "perspicuous overview" of its uses, and thus gain some insight into the relevant resemblances with which we ought to be concerned. Once this is accomplished we may then go on to employ the same analysis to identify good and bad political trials.

NOTES

1. The methods of the following analysis are modeled after that in H. R. Van Gunsteren, *The Quest for Control: A Critique of the Rational-Central Rule Approach in Public Affairs* (New York: John Wiley & Sons, 1976).

2. See any number of introductory or advanced texts, e.g., D. Brody, *The American Legal System* (Lexington, MA: D. C. Heath Co., 1978), 3–7; H. J. Berman, *The Nature and Function of Law* (Brooklyn, NY: The Foundation Press, 1958), 20–28; M. P. Goulding, ed., *The Nature of Law* (New York: Random House, 1966).

3. T. Aquinas, "Law as an Ordinance of Reason," in Goulding, *The Nature of Law,* 12–13.

4. T. Hobbes, *Leviathan* (New York: Washington Square Press, 1964), 188.

5. See J. Austin, *The Province of Jurisprudence Determined,* in Goulding, *The Nature of Law* 73–98; H.L.A. Hart, *The Concept of Law* (New York: Oxford University Press, 1961); and H. Kelson, *General Theory of Law and State* (Cambridge: Harvard University Press, 1945).

6. For an excellent, detailed account about rules, see "Following a Rule: A Philosophical Analysis," in Van Gunsteren, *The Quest for Control,* 113–120.

7. L. Wittgenstein, *Remarks on the Foundations of Mathematics* (New York: Oxford University Press, 1967), 34.

8. Ibid., 217.

9. For an interesting analysis of law as a process of balancing policies and principles, see R. M. Dworkin, "Is Law a System and Rules?" in R. M. Dworkin, ed., *The Philosophy of Law* (New York: Oxford University Press, 1977), 38–82.

10. For an extensive treatment of this issue, see K. H. Wolff, ed., *The Sociology of George Simmel* (Glencoe, IL: The Free Press, 1950), 181–186.

11. Wittgenstein, *Foundation of Mathematics*, xi.

12. Ibid., xii, xiii.

13. Ibid., para. 401.

14. Ibid., para. 66 and 67.

15. T. L. Becker, *Political Trials* (Indianapolis, IN: Bobbs-Merrill, 1971), xii.

16. Ibid.

17. Ibid.

18. Ibid.

19. Ibid., xiii.

20. Wittgenstein, *Foundation of Mathematics*, xii.

21. Becker, *Political Trials*, xii.

22. J. Rawls, *A Theory of Justice* (Cambridge: Harvard University Press, 1971), 383.

23. N. Dorsen and L. Friedman, *Disorder in the Court* (New York: Pantheon Books, 1973), ch. 5.

24. Ibid., 79.

25. Ibid., 87.

26. Ibid., 78.

27. O. Kirchheimer, *Political Justice: The Use of Legal Procedure for Political Ends* (Princeton, NJ: Princeton University Press, 1961), 6.

28. Ibid., 46.

29. Ibid., 49.

30. Dorsen and Friedman, *Disorder*, 78.

31. See F. D. Allen, *The Crimes of Politics: Political Dimensions of Criminal Justice* (Cambridge: Harvard University Press, 1974), 52.

32. L. Wittgenstein, *Tractatus Logico-Philosophicus* (London: Routledge and Kegan Paul, 1961), para. 4.021.

33. Ibid., 4.024.

34. L. Wittgenstein, *Philosophical Investigations* (New York: MacMillan Publishing Co., 1953). para. 66–67.

35. Allen, *Crimes of Politics*, 43.

36. Ibid., 27.

37. Ibid., 33.

38. Ibid., 42.

39. Ibid., 43.

40. Ibid.

41. D. Volkan, "The Need to Have Enemies and Allies: A Developmental Approach," 6 *Political Psychology* 2 (1985), 219–248.

42. Ibid.

Chapter Three

Defining and Evaluating Political Trials

To this point we have demonstrated the problematic nature of our endeavor to define and evaluate political trials. The nature of a trial as well as its goodness or badness is tied intimately and inextricably to changing social and political events. Nevertheless, we have also argued that it is not impossible to define and evaluate political trials. It is, however, a difficult and complex undertaking that cannot be encapsulated in naturalist or positivist terms. This chapter demonstrates a method of analyzing numerous examples of the intimate relationship between court decisions and their context and deriving an assessment of the "politicalness" of trials and an evaluation of their goodness.

Our analysis so far indicates that to really understand what is meant by "political trial" we must begin by obtaining a "perspicuous overview" of how "political trial" is used. It is not possible nor necessary to be exhaustive in our examples. The examples we use are not model cases to be held up to other situations as a sort of template nor is "political trial" the sum total of the characteristic uses of the term. Our examples are simply places to begin, suggesting some widely considered traits of political trials.

Similarly, the characteristics that we suggest mark good or bad political trials are meant to be neither exhaustive nor absolute. They are signs of bad political trials, for example, only because of our order, our institutions, our political and economic ways of operating, and our strategies for pursuing desired ends and securing certain values. Trials are critiqued in terms of who we are now. We must ask, "What is intolerable to us? What makes us wince? What ignites our indignation? What is our 'regime of truth?' " What is our understanding of the proper order and the proper dynamic for the production, regulation, distribution, circulation, and operation of power? Trials are not understood as bad on the basis of a principle, paradigm, institution, or set of values apart from our practice. They are bad because their statements, logics, rationales, or values violate that system of ordered procedures constituting our principles of discourse and devised especially for the production of true statements about power.

USES OF "POLITICAL TRIAL"

Perhaps the classical use of "political trial" occurs where governments attempt to eliminate individuals or groups they perceive as threats to their power.[1] The trials of Socrates for corrupting Athenian youth, Jesus Christ for sedition, Sir Thomas More for malicious silence regarding the king's religious hegemony, and the special trials of those attacking the Nazi government in Germany between 1933 and 1934, clearly fall under this use. Similarly, trials aimed at large numbers of people, such as those of the Spanish Inquisition, are of this sort, as are trials aimed at specific groups (such as, the Rosenberg trial as an example of anticommunism). Trials are useful tools in such situations because they can legitimize the elimination of a foe so far as the public at large is concerned.

Another use of political trials, very similar to the first, occurs when courts are used as organs of political struggle. That is, they are not just employed to oppress or eliminate opponents, but are used in whatever way possible to establish, secure, and expand the power of those in government. Examples of this type of political trial include those held after the Russian Revolution and during the Stalin era. Though the courts were used in these instances to eliminate political foes, the main thrust of such trials was to attain the political goals and promote the political values of those in power. In the words of the Russian prosecutor-general, the courts were "an organ of the class struggle of the workers directed against their enemies . . . in the interests of the revolution . . . having in mind the most desirable results for the masses of workers and peasants."[2] Less obvious but nevertheless clear instances of this type of political trial are provided by certain early cases in the U.S. Supreme Court, which established the right of federal courts to review the decisions of state courts[3] and generally enhanced the power of the national government over that of the states. Such decisions went a long way toward establishing the substantive principles upon which present American policy concerning the federal/state relationship rests.[4]

A third use of political trials occurs when courts use their decisions to establish, secure, and expand their power as an institution vis-a-vis other governmental institutions (e.g., the executive and legislative branches) or the power of the governmental institutions over private citizens or states.[5] A prime example of this type of trial is *Marbury v. Madison*,[6] in which the

U.S. Supreme Court arrogated to itself the power of judicial review over the other two branches of government. In addition to *Marbury*, attempts to use the civil and criminal law to enforce the interests of one branch of government over the others or over private citizens include the affirmation of congressional power to restrict federal appellate jurisdiction in *Ex Parte McCardle*,[7] and the trial of the "Catonsville Nine," in which the defendants claimed, *inter alia*, that the government was acting *ultra vires* in its prosecution of the Vietnam war.[8] Generally, it is understood that courts have interests in maintaining their sovereignty and independence in the face of challenges from other political institutions and regularly use their discretion in choosing cases and in framing the issues to secure these ends.

A fourth use of political trials is in situations where a prosecution is used to split up mass movements or prevent them from gathering momentum by (1) singling out individuals for public deprecation during a trial (e.g., the conspiracy prosecutions of "The Chicago Seven"); (2) frightening off potential followers by the threat of possible prosecution; and (3) promoting dissention in the ranks of a movement either by offering immunity to those who will turn state's evidence against other members or portraying the leaders of certain groups in the movement as dangerous, perverse, or thoughtless. An example of this type of political trial was that concerning the murder of the newly elected Kentucky governor of 1899.[9] The governor was a Democrat, and the accused murderer was a prominent exponent of the Republican Party, which had been gaining more and more political support. It was apparent at the time that control of the state hung in the balance. The Democrats proceeded to link the killing of the governor-elect to an alleged plot hatched by the Republican Party. The point was to convince the electorate that the entire Republican Party should stand convicted of murder.

Political trials have also been used where certain patterns of prosecution result from deliberate policy choices by governmental institutions that structure into our political, social, or commercial spheres certain types of crime as responses to certain kinds of advantage or disadvantage. An example would be the trials for rum-running during Prohibition in the United States. In this situation, a particular group gained control of the legal mechanisms of a society and established a set of rules effectively calling for the systematic prosecution of a life style embodying a different set of values.

More broadly, deliberate policy choices normally create social or economic problems for certain people because of their social or economic position. When such policies also restrict options for dealing with these problems and constrain decisions about which options to adopt, they go a long way toward making criminality a rational (or at least a reasonable) career choice.[10] Actually, a number of such problems and constraints are structured into our legal system, and some of them are not immediately apparent, although they have undeniable political effects.

Consider, for example, the criteria for probation established by the California Sentencing Institute in 1965.[11] The criteria include (1) no excessive contempt for property rights, (2) loyalty to his or her employer, (3) regular church attendance, and (4) active engagement "in civic improvement organizations." There is a political philosophy behind these criteria and those who are not of that philosophical bent will not be released from California jails. These criteria propound the philosophy of Locke with its stress on the sacredness of property rights and its conviction that the hand of God is at work supporting civic action that reflects those rights. But this philosophy is so deeply buried that most people are not conscious that a philosophy is even there at all. It is simply the case, for most, that respect for property, employers, church, and civic organizations are indicative of responsible citizenship regardless of the nature of the individuals who may be occupying those positions or the values those people may be promoting. What we call the "American way of life" is a "nationalist articulation of Locke which usually does not know that Locke himself is involved." Ours is a "society which began with Locke" and "stays with Locke, by virtue of an absolute and irrational attachment to his principles."[12] Those among us who are not consciously or unconsciously Lockean are in subtle jeopardy.

Again, political trial is often used in situations where a crime has been committed for political purposes, and the defendants seek to benefit from the publicity of the trial either by affecting the behavior of the prosecution (thereby making the "accuser" look evil or incompetent) or by using the trial as a forum for publicizing their political views and values. Additionally, defendants in this type of trial may attempt to use the court to try certain government policies. Examples of this type of political trial include the "Catonsville Nine" (destroying selective service draft records during the Vietnam War),[13] the 1916 trial of Fredrich Adler for the murder of the Austrian Prime Minister[14] (Adler maintained throughout the trial that his act was moral because the First World War which the Prime Minister supported and pursued was illegal and inhuman), and the trial of Karl Armstrong for bombing the Army Math Research Center at the University of Wisconsin in 1970 (his act was directed against the Vietnam War and his hearing became, in effect, a trial of that war).

Finally, "political trial" can be used when there is an intense, vociferous, or widespread public outcry against certain political figures because of their conduct in office to satisfy the general outrage or to redress the imbalance of power that allowed the conduct in the first place. This type of political trial can take three forms. First, an important economic or social group might be intensely outraged at either the conduct of certain individuals or groups within government or the conduct of the government as a whole toward them or others with whom they are sympathetic. Examples include such welfare rights cases as *Goldberg v. Kelly*, in which public assistance payments were terminated without an evidentiary hearing.[15] Second, the general public might be angry or cynical about either the government as a whole or certain political groups because of their abuse of a government's power. Examples include Watergate, Abscam, and the Teapot Dome scandal. Third, whole societies or even a number of societies might be outraged by the conduct of a government as a whole. Examples include the Nuremburg trials and the various international conventions on genocide, human rights, and racial equality that hold out the promise that international tribunals may hear cases involving a government's coercion or oppression of its own people.[16]

Now that we have provided an overview of the concept's use, we will illustrate characteristics among these individual uses. Then we can identify the implications of our analysis and the sophisticated understanding of "political trials" in light of whether or not such trials are justified and how political trials might be used to redress the imbalances of social and political power reflected in court decisions. To begin, we will identify the characteristics of the uses mentioned earlier and their cases, that would reasonably lead us to evaluate the political trial as "bad." Then we will do the same for evaluating the trial as "good," and end by outlining some implications of this analysis, which will be detailed in the following chapter.

Before we begin, though, it is worth repeating that what is to follow is not intended to provide exhaustive criteria for identifying the many kinds of political trials. Nor is it intended to capture the fundamental essence of the good or bad in politics or law. We think all of that impossible. Rather, we intend to point out certain resemblances among what we within our order generally and currently mean when we use the terms "good" and "bad" while operating with reference to the linguistic and intellectual regimes of politics and law. We will note what is viewed as good or bad now, within our current networks of legal and political relationships; given our current struggles, strategies, and tactics; and according to our current forms of knowledge and our current discourse. We will present examples not to illustrate the application of set principles or rules but as both illustrative events in the process of change and as practices which themselves alter the order of things. We intend to show how it is that as we act through our courts to circulate power, we change not only our order, our discourse and our strategies but also our values, goals and ideas of what counts as truth. Finally, we intend to show how the changes trials work are not incoherent, arbitrary, capricious or absurd as a result of being political but are intelligible and meaningful in terms of the practices constituting the order worked out in practice, case by case.

CHARACTERISTICS OF BAD POLITICAL TRIALS

Black and White Thinking and the Common Enemy

One prominent characteristic of a bad political trial is the tendency to employ black and white thinking. Black and white thinking identifies a definable group as the embodiment of everything worth hating, in contrast with that which is acceptable. Once identified, the group and all of its individual members are fair game and bagging one or all of them becomes a civic duty. This is a trait of bad political trials simply because politics is concerned primarily with group behavior, and it is most important that those human passions that drive people together be employed properly to bring the collectivity to desired political ends.

Appeals to fear, for example, are often the most expedient of devices for co-ordinating and directing corrective action. Politicians observed a long time ago that appeals to fear require someone to hate. They also observed that we love those who hate our enemies for correctly identifying and properly oppressing those deserving of our hatred. This explains the relish with which many of us vilify our enemies: It serves the psychological need to identify concretely what we fear, hate it, punish it, and in the process love ourselves and one another for doing so.

Sane and intelligent people, once occupied with satisfying this impulse, will engage in behavior any detached observer would think irrational. During the McCarthy era, for example, Chief Justice Frederick Vinson hated Communists so strongly, because they did not allow liberty, that he decided to imitate them. During his tenure, rights to assembly, free press, and free speech were methodically eliminated through a proper construction of the Smith Act in order to secure America against a threat to democracy from the Communist Party USA. As his former law clerk recalled, "If those guys were Communists . . . those were not tough decisions for him."[17] This was the height of the cold war and Vinson had come to the court from a wartime administration. He "still thought like a man mobilizing America for a struggle against the nation's enemies. Decisions involving Communists were for him a foregone conclusion."[18]

How is this allowed to happen? Its genesis lies in the fact, recognized as early as Aristotle. Interwoven with many other political motives is the human need to establish well-defined groups with shared goals and mutual concerns. The Greek *polis* was understood as an expression of this need and of the character of the people who made it up. Through this expression, the polis gave identity to the Greeks by pointing out the similarities of its members and the differences of those who did not belong.

This identification with one group and the distinguishing of another is not necessarily bad. It secures two indispensable prerequisites to human progress: conflict and co-operation. Co-operation is necessary because none of us is born complete and self-sufficient. At some point we must trust others, and to trust them, we must feel that they are good and like ourselves. Conflict, too, is one source of growth. To be handled well, it requires change and self-examination; consequently, a little conflict is desirable.

Conflict is also important because, as Michel Foucault chronicles in many of his works, there is always something in the individual and in society that escapes the network of power. There is a quality or aspect of individuals or groups that responds to every advance of power by inertia, countermovement, or disengagement. So where there is power there is resistance, and to efficiently circulate power, to get things done, to produce things and to form knowledge, we must handle that resistance well. We must properly integrate, subjugate, utilize, or stabilize that resistance in ways that do the least violence to our goals, values, and ability to operate as the kind of society we want to be.

Conflict, however, is often handled poorly. While it is normal for us to invest our particular group with all of the best qualities, it is also normal for us to turn this around and invest outsiders with responsibility for all the evils that we experience.[19] This tends to harden our position and to encourage a kind of regression into primitive horde behavior when we are under stress.[20] If the out group, for example, is evil, out of control, and only respects force, we feel justified in using force against them, and they, in turn, feel justified in using force against us, as they often see us in the same terms as we see them. In this way, each group satisfies its own occasional desire to be out of control and ensures that its own display of violence is both righteous and noble.[21]

Before long, each group becomes dependent on having a stable, accessible enemy constituting a suitable embodiment of all the feelings and behaviors we have negated in ourselves as evil, treacherous, warlike, and cruel. Regularly trouncing on what we perceive as the less laudable attributes of others is a convenient way of continually affirming our own identity as trustworthy, peace loving, honorable, and humanitarian. We need an enemy good enough to serve as a ready contrast with our own group, to provide a negative identity for our positive one, and to help us develop a distinct sense of ourselves. So if we do not have a proper enemy at hand, it is often necessary to find one.

The courts have not been slackers in this regard. At the beginning of our political history, the favorite judicial approach was to cast dissenters in the role of blasphemers in league with the devil, as was done in the sedition trial of John Peter Zenger. During this century, the courts repeatedly exhibited similar behavior resulting from the anxiety that American civilization was soon to be turned upside down by a centrally organized, brilliantly directed, well-financed, and devilishly insidious Russian conspiracy on American shores, which in fact did not exist. Such was the occasion for the *Dennis* case in which Justice Vinson played so prominent a role,[22] and earlier this century, it was the occasion for the famous trio of *Schenck, Frohwerk,* and *Debs*,[23] punishing people for leafletting, writing newspaper articles, and making speeches against the First World War.

More recently, this same behavior was evident in the case of *U.S. v. Dellinger, et al.*[24] In this case, seven antiwar activists—each representative of different groups of people, all of whom opposed the Vietnam war but some of whom had never before seen each other—were charged with conspiring to disrupt the 1968 Democratic National Convention. This prosecution was a transparent attempt to portray the antiwar movement as the orchestrated machination of forces within our own population determined to bring down our American way of life.[25] At Present, Middle Eastern terrorists and Third World revolutionaries are the newest group of devils. Organized, dedicated, and fiendishly clever, they are seriously presented as having first been part of the international communist conspiracy directed from Moscow but now simply crazed by either a false religious or social consciousness or the drive for power and money and making dupes of many naive and unrealistic people, not unlike those in the early trials of this genre.

A prudent regard for our national security is undeniably a healthy thing. So, we must carefully distinguish the cases just mentioned from trials such as *Agee* which, as we have argued, was a good political trial punishing someone through the civil law for employing speech and press in a way demonstrably abusive of his rights under the Constitution. But that case does not resemble these in that they do not involve the attempt by government to create or exploit an out group for political purposes

Conspiracy

A second characteristic is the tendency of bad political trials to exaggerate the danger of the wrongdoing that they are intended to curb. This is illustrated by the use of conspiracy to establish the prosecution's case. In fact, the conspiracy indictment is probably the most certain sign that the danger is being exaggerated. If the danger were real, there would most probably be a tangible wrong to try rather than this inchoate offense.

Conspiracy is an inchoate offense because it does not require that anything illegal be done. It only requires that people agree to do it, and courts have shown a natural disposition to infer agreement from the fact that the accused belonged to an "out group," such as Communists or antiwar activists.[26] During the Smith Act prosecutions of the 1950s, for example, the government indictments charged defendants with conspiracy, and the prosecutors extensively described the underground and clandestine fulminations of the Communist Party so as to stress its conspirational nature.[27] The most damaging evidence in these trials regularly turned out to be hearsay testimony concerning what Communists other than the defendants had to say about party purposes and goals. The core of the prosecution's case was either such hearsay or the insistence that the defendants were mindlessly following a Marxist-Leninist line, without deviation and without regard for circumstance, history, or their own critical reason.[28]

In reality, if Communists or any other group were as intent upon lawlessness as they were said to be, there was an adequate body of criminal law to cope with their actual misdeeds. It was not necessary to attack their rights to speech, free press, and assembly. If the threatening group does not violate any existing prohibitions, perhaps they are not all that menacing. The only way that these cases can be seen as a rational reaction is to assume that they represent an anticipatory or preventative approach to crime justified by what the troublemakers stand for or what their speech suggests. These cases make it quite clear that punishing people for what they might do in the future, or for the possible ramifications of their speech, has proven an attractive and enduring motive for prosecution.

More recently, the *Snepp* and *Agee* cases revealed much the same strategy. Prosecutors in these cases sought, with fair success, to cast the defendants as either unwitting dupes or comrades-in-arms with international terrorist organizations. These cases are interesting because of the speculative nature of the damages that the government sought to prove. The *Snepp* case, for example, found that disclosures by former CIA agents were harmful to vital national interests even if the disclosed information was unclassified. The finding was explicitly based on CIA Director Stanfield Turner's testimony (which the court forbade the defense to cross-examine) that

I cannot estimate to you how many potential sources or liaison arrangements have never germinated because people were unwilling to enter business with us.[29]

This was as close as the government came to demonstrable evidence of harm to the national security. But it does illustrate the increased deference given to official perspectives and interpretations that we find in political trials of the nastiest sort.

Consider, for example, the case of *Goldman v. Weinberger*.[30] Officer Goldman, a clinical psychologist at the U.S. Air Force base in Riverside, California, testified most effectively as a defense witness at a court marshall. At the end of Goldman's testimony, the prosecutor complained to the court that Goldman's yarmulke violated Air Force regulations. The Supreme Court agreed because "courts must give great deference to the professional judgment of military authorities concerning the relative importance of a particular military interest." Somehow, the military was arguing, Officer Goldman's yarmulke reduced the military's ability to "provide an effective defense on a moment's notice, by undermining discipline, reflexive compliance with battlefield orders, and esprit de corps." As Justice William Brennan said in dissent, "Today the court eschews its constitutionally mandated role. It adopts for review of military decisions a subrational basis standard—absolute, uncritical deference to the professional judgment of military authorities." Like the *Joyner* case and its progeny studied in chapter 1, the *Goldman* case is about authority relationships, not the national defense. It is about politics at home and not battlefield behavior, and it is about our general aversion to eccentricity and the personal frustration we feel when the eccentric among us bests us on our own turf. The First Amendment suffered here, especially the right to practice freely our religion, and it suffered needlessly under the circumstances.

Once again, the cases we have just considered must be carefully distinguished from those cases in which the danger is much more palpable, such as *Agee* and *Dombrowski*. In *Dombrowski* there was in fact a conspiracy— a conspiracy by public officials not to break the law but only to use the law to frustrate people in the exercise of their First Amendment freedoms. In *Agee*, too, there was a conspiracy between the Passport Office and the CIA to pull a dangerous man within the jurisdiction of our national courts, although they lacked the legal foundation to do so. Certainly we can find as much of a "constructive agreement" here as courts found in *Dellinger, Dennis*, and *Whitney* and we can find considerably more behavior in pursuit of that agreement. In both cases, the conspiring parties made no attempt to deny either element of the offense. Rather, they put forward their actions as the patriotic duty of those invested with the public trust, allowing the court to play its peculiar role in democratic government. The court decided that the activities in *Dombrowski* were not so patriotic after all, but that those in *Agee* were. In so doing, it altered the balance of power and promoted change in one instance, while defending the nation's security in the other— both laudatory results arrived at in the most principled way practicable under the circumstances.

The Appeal to Emotion

This characteristic of bad political trials is probably best illustrated by the use of what we call "erotico-thanotopic imagery," which are words that subliminally excite sensuous responses, juxtaposed or intertwined with images of death that are often associated with pernicious, spreading disease.[31] Such imagery exerts a particularly debilitating force on the critical faculties of human beings, stimulating even clear-headed people to do things they otherwise would not.[32] We find this sort of imagery used in bad political trials in order to short circuit reason and stimulate us to the uncritical pursuit of questionable social policy.

Fire is one image that captures this complex of interrelated feelings. Fire is heat, excitement, warmth, passion, and death. It is the abode of Satan and the sword of God ("He hath loosed the fateful lightning of His terrible, swift sword"). It speaks of purification, death, and evil. It is erotic ("burning love," "light my fire"), mesmerizing, fearful, and attractive ("like a moth to a flame").

Judges use this image in political trials all the time. "The most stringent protection of free speech would not protect a man falsely shouting fire in a theater and causing a panic," wrote Justice Holmes in the *Schenck* case.[33] "A little breath would be enough to kindle a flame," said Holmes again in *Frohwerk*,[34] and Justice Vinson evoked the "inflammable nature of world conditions" in *Dennis*.[35] Perhaps the most interesting example is the question posed by Chief Justice Morrison Waite in *Reynolds v. United States*,[36] in which the court disallowed polygamy among Mormons: "If a wife religiously believed it was her duty to burn herself upon the funeral pile of her dead husband, would it be beyond the power of the civil government to prevent her carrying her belief into practice?" He clearly considered the question both rhetorical and dispositive of the issue. The image was meant to put an end to argument; in his own mind it appears not only to have ended all argument, but all reason and self-criticism that good argument involves. Consequently, we are justified in characterizing his conclusions as merely arbitrary and so bad law.

Fire, of course, is not the only clear image in this regard. Later on in *Reynolds*, Justice Waite provides another image. In upholding as non-prejudicial the trial judge's charge to the jury, Justice Waite said the following:

You should consider what are to be the consequences to the innocent victims of this delusion. As this contest goes on they multiply, and there are pure minded women and there are innocent children; innocent in a sense even beyond the degree of the innocence of childhood itself. These are to be the sufferers; and as jurors fail to do their duty, and as these cases come up in the territory of Utah, just so do these victims multiply and spread themselves over the land.[37]

Here we have the image of polygamy spreading like a disease over the land. It spreads through the women, and it causes the death of innocence, purity, and any notion of goodness beyond the mundane. Eros and Thanatos are well blended here to overwhelm both our reason and our tolerance.

The image of death often serves the same purpose. Political leaders can "catalyze organized violence in mass audiences by symbolizing political . . . death in the signs and symbols of ritual tragic drama."[38] More simply: Politics is communal drama and the central political drama is the struggle of good against evil. In this struggle, death plays a central role. The threat of death from the enemy and our need to purify society of evil by killing the enemy are two things that justify a political hierarchy.

Images of death and struggle are often employed to evoke the necessary social support for politically repressive trials. "When a nation is at war," said Justice Holmes, "many things that might be said in times of peace are such a hindrance to its effort that their utterance will not be endured so long as men fight."[39] The idea seems to be that First Amendment freedoms must die so that the nation might live. This proposition was taken as indisputable in *U.S. v. The Progressive*.[40] This was a case prosecuted by the government to enjoin the publication of technical information on the hydrogen bomb—information garnered from a vast array of public sources and focused on how the bomb is constructed and how it works. Without an evidentiary hearing, the judge concluded that the article posed a grave danger to national security and enjoined publication. On the free press issue, the court said, "There is a hierarchy of values attached to these rights . . . one cannot enjoy freedom of speech . . . or freedom of the press unless one enjoys the freedom to live."[41]

Justice Felix Frankfurter expressed this same sentiment in *Minersville School District v. Gobitus*,[42] when he ordered a twelve-year-old girl and her ten-year-old brother to salute the flag every day in school despite their religious conviction that the flag was a graven image and not to be so honored under pain of eternal damnation. He justified this by pointing out that the "ultimate foundation of a free society is the binding tie of cohesive sentiment," and that the flag "is the symbol of our national unity" signifying "absolute safety for free institutions against foreign aggression." So, once again, for reasons of national security the First Amendment was circumvented.

While *Gobitus* was overruled three years later because "compulsory unification of opinion achieves only the unanimity of the graveyard,"[43] the general sentiment survives as evinced in the *Goldberg* case, in which the Supreme Court found it necessary to national security that an orthodox Jew not be permitted to wear his yarmulke while in uniform. Military authority must "foster instinctive obedience, unity, commitment and esprit de corps," said Justice William Rhenquist, and four other justices agreed.[44]

Free exercise of religion and free speech guarantees are not the only things that have suffered under the creative use of death imagery. In holding that a child could not be permitted to distribute religious tracts on street corners with his or her mother, the Supreme Court made it clear that the family is not beyond regulation in the public interest and that "neither rights of religion nor rights of parenthood are beyond limitation." The right of a parent to control a child's behavior, even under the claim of free exercise of religion, "does not include liberty to expose the community or the child to communicable disease or the latter to ill health or death."[45] This is, of course, incontestable. It was also irrelevant to the case that involved parents directly supervising their children in distributing pamphlets, without the slightest indication of danger to the child's health, safety, or welfare. Here, the specter of death and disease was raised solely to overcome the facts.

This same sort of imagery, however, has on occasion been used to secure First Amendment guarantees. Justice Holmes, for example, wrote a dissenting opinion in *Abrams v. U.S.*,[46] arguing that "we should be eternally vigilant against attempts to check the expression of opinions that we loathe and believe to be fraught with death,"[47] and he tried to substitute the metaphor of a "marketplace of ideas" for those of death and fire used in earlier cases. But although this imagery eventually dominated, that accomplishment is not very comforting. Reasoned argument and analysis are comforting in these situations, not the hope that we might provide the right metaphor.

Guilt by Association or Inference

Everyone has experienced the irritation of listening to neighbors, news commentators, or the more popular television evangelists, knowing that they do not know what they are talking about. The impulse is to intervene and set matters straight. But when you begin to formulate a response, you realize that they are so profoundly confused that you would have to start with first principles, the relevance of which they would not immediately perceive, and that their education is more than you have the time or inclination to accomplish.

One currently popular form of argument, for example, is to seek support for one's position by denouncing people who do not agree with you, as Communists, demagogues, terrorists, secular humanists, and, most recently, liberals. Most people, however, do not actually know what the words *communist, secular humanist,* or *liberal* mean, and so they are too easily frightened into believing that they denote every imaginable extremity. The word *communist,* for example, has a negative connotation to most Americans, although really it means nothing more than one who thinks we should all live after the manner of Christ and his immediate disciples as they wandered about the desert at the beginning of his ministry. And *capitalist,* a very popular word at the moment, means nothing more than one who believes in the self-organizing anarchy of an open market. The essence of this approach to political debate is simply to defeat the opponent by association and inference.

This approach is a hallmark of the bad political trial. *Whitney v. California*[48] is the archetypal trial using this approach when free speech is involved, and *Davis v. Beason*[49] is a parallel free exercise case. Anna Whitney was convicted of attending a Communist Labor Party convention, which adopted a platform urging "revolutionary unionism." She was convicted under a statute making it a crime to advocate the desirability or necessity of violence in social and political change, even though she was expressly present at the convention to oppose any such platform and spoke vociferously against any such behavior. The court simply reasoned that since she belonged to an organization that, through the adoption of a "revolutionary unionism" platform, advocated the necessity of violence, she must be guilty of such sentiments herself.

In the same way, Samuel Davis was convicted for conspiring to "pervert and obstruct the due administration of the laws of the territory of Idaho." As a member of the Mormon Church, he swore a statutorily required oath before election registrars that he was neither a bigamist nor polygamist nor a member of an association teaching, advising, or encouraging bigamy or polygamy. In fact, he was not a practicing polygamist and there was no evidence outside his Mormon Church membership suggesting that he personally supported polygamy as a tenant of his faith (the polygamist Mormons at that time were one faction of the church originally founded by Joseph Smith). His membership alone was enough to convict.

Since *Whitney* and *Davis* attained convictions based on statutes making nothing more than membership in organizations advocating different and unpopular ideas a sufficient ground for conviction (regardless of personal behavior and belief), such statutes became popular devices. State legislatures adjourned their 1950 sessions, for example, after passing over 300 enactments ascribing criminal propensities to groups (usually but not exclusively Communists) and ascribing criminality to any individual linked with such groups.[50] A federal statute of this type was responsible for the conviction, in *Dennis v. U.S.*,[51] of the national board of the Communist Party on conspiracy charges, which were proven by the testimony of informers concerning what other party members, not on trial, had said to the witnesses on various occasions about the goals and purposes of the Communist Party.[52]

Just as inflated estimates of the danger are linked with conspiracy charges, guilt by association and inference is most efficiently expressed and prosecuted through the same medium. This is not fortuitous. Under conspiracy law, statements made by any alleged coconspirator can be attributed to each coconspirator, acts by any one member within the scope of the conspiracy are equally attributable to all members of the conspiracy, the acts and the statements can be established by hearsay, and the necessary agreement and intent can be inferred from the same circumstantial evidence by speculating on what people acting in a certain way must have had in mind.[53] So once a political party is understood to be a conspiracy, one can be vicariously liable for anything another party member says or does under the banner of party activity.

The seductive effect that this tactic has on prosecutors who can project an agreement and the necessary intent for a crime on independently acting individuals acting in new and different ways is perhaps best illustrated by the already detailed tactic of charging civil rights workers in the South with criminal conspiracy under various state subversive activities and Communist control laws during the 1960s.[54] But no less captivating is the use of conspiracy charges against the "Boston Five," charged with conspiracy to counsel, aid, and abet violations of the selective service law and to hinder the administration of the draft during the Vietnam War. These five individuals somehow constituted a cabal, in the government's eyes, because they had independently attended the same functions in different combinations:

How did these five wind up as accused conspirators? They hardly knew each other. . . . When for the first time all five met together—after the indictment, in attorney Leonard Boudin's living room, to discuss their common plight—Boudin says the first thing he felt he could do for these conspirators was to introduce them to each other.[55]

Obviously, we cannot underestimate the heights of subtlety that can be reached in attributing guilt by association and inference.

LEGAL MORALISM

One enduring source of the bad political trial is the idea that one's moral duty as a citizen requires deference to established authority and its interpretation of events. As we have seen, the enforcement of the required deference is often justified by overestimating the dangers that either face us directly or are thought to result from a lack of deference. They are a warning to those who, plumed with an overwrought sense of honesty or indignation, would hover above the government and criticize its shortcomings. It is a warning that at some point the public good requires silence, and as far as the government is concerned, that point is usually when the criticisms strike most closely to home.

Another way of silencing the over intense is to assume a uniform idea of moral behavior according to a fixed image of a proper social order and then to enforce that order by casting every criticism of it as not only traitorous but immoral. This, of course, justifies twisting the law to reach obviously wrong conduct, even if there is no law or legal theory remotely on point.

One device that the federal courts are presently experimenting with toward accomplishing this end is the constructive trust. In *U.S. v. Snepp* the court imposed a constructive trust on any profits from the sale of *Decent Interval* after finding that Frank Snepp had breached his contract not to publish without CIA approval when he pulled together prepublished and unclassified material into a single volume.[56] Although the appellate court set aside the trust as an unwarranted restriction on First Amendment rights,[57] the Supreme Court had it reinstated. The purpose of this trust was "simply to require him to disgorge the benefits of his faithlessness."[58]

Constructive trusts are equitable remedies arising whenever circumstances make it inequitable that property should be retained by the holder of legal title. Here, the court argued that Snepp should not keep his money because he was unfaithful to the CIA by making them look bad through his criticism. Without a hearing and without taking briefs, Snepp was consigned to perdition, the First Amendment notwithstanding, as the Court went on to indicate that even without the contract Snepp signed agreeing to CIA oversight, he would have been sanctioned.[59] The Court clearly means us to understand that fidelity to government institutions is a higher moral duty for the citizen than the public discussion of critical issues.

The moral responsibilities were said to be the other way around in 1964 when the Supreme Court declared in *Near v. Minnesota*[60] that "criticism of . . . official conduct does not lose its constitutional protection merely because it is effective."[61] Similarly, in the "Pentagon Papers" case,[62] the Court said that the whole point of the First Amendment was to disallow punishment for talk "embarrassing to the powers that be," since "secrecy in government is fundamentally anti-democratic."[63] Our history, however, indicates that when our leaders call for discipline, order, silence, patriotism, and devotion to the state, we respond enthusiastically. The practical tendency in our democracy seems to be the implementation of the idea that public work should be done by patriotic persons invested with sufficient coercive authority to uproot the inefficiency of interest group politics and replace it with virtuous, energetic, and clear-thinking minions blessed with an unmuddled vision of what makes America great. Nothing interferes with this dynamic more, nor more insidiously eats away at public unity and resolve, than critical malcontents and demagogues who gain a public platform. As their behavior threatens to reinstate the confusion and corruption from which we have been rescued, some means consistent with our democratic ideals must be found to keep them quiet. Our analysis so far has chronicled a bevy of legal devices toward this end, including seditious libel, summary arrest and detention, espionage acts, anti-Communist laws, and constructive trusts.

THE UNIQUENESS OF POLITICAL TRIALS

An implicit theme running through everything we have said so far is that there seems to be an unmistakable quality about political trials that separates them from ordinary trials and that focuses on the public questioning of whether the government is doing the right thing with the proper concern for human rights. An acute intuition about this difference has always existed parallel to the trials themselves.

Following the Civil War, for example, the thorny problem of what to do about citizens who adhered patriotically to the Southern cause needed to be addressed. Those citizens supported the South because that was where they were born, that was where their friends were, and that was where they had built their lives. They were, however, traitors. But somehow their motives were clearly more elevated than those manifested by the common criminal, and the nature of the rights they violated were distinguishable as well.

Similarly, following the Second World War, a lively public debate broke out about the continuing imprisonment of those convicted of obstructing the war effort. They were convicted criminals under the Espionage Act, and they were also anarchists, socialists, and International Workers of the World. But to many they were prisoners of conscience, neither motivated by the self-serving goals that hallmark the ordinary criminal, nor seeking the ignoble ends of everyday crime.

Finally, during the Vietnam War and the civil rights movement, acts in contravention of the criminal law were often associated with the resistance and the struggle for equality. Somehow, again, there was a recognizable dignity to many of those criminal acts and though many did not share the values or the sense of urgency of either the resistance or the movement, most could recognize the impulse behind those criminal acts as something apart from what we ordinarily recognize as criminal intent.

This peculiarity of political trials has long been recognized by foreign writers. Robert Ferrari, for example, points out that "political crime is not a natural crime. It is dependent upon the legislature, and differs considerably from place to place. It is still more varied than common statutory crime."[64] He goes on to quote Vidal, the French authority on criminal law:

If . . . the political criminal is reprehensible and ought to be punished in the interest of the established order, his criminality cannot be compared with that of the ordinary malefactor, with the murderer, the thief, etc. The criminality has not at all the same immorality. It is only relative, dependent on time, place, and circumstances, the institutions of the land, and it is often inspired by noble sentiments, by disinterested motives, by devotion to persons and principles, by love of one's country.[65]

We are not arguing, after all that we have said, that there is a core concept to which all ideas about political trials may be reduced. We are only pointing out that two of our most important social practices are involved in political trials as opposed to ordinary criminal trials: (1) the practice of worrying about whether we are doing the right thing, and (2) the practice of worrying about this publicly. The second practice necessarily includes the concomitant traditions of protecting constitutionally the freedoms of speech, press, and association. The recognition that these practices are involved alters the common perception of these trials in different ways at different times, but always in such a manner as to make their distinctiveness apparent. When either the plaintiff or the defendant has acted with a concern for justice and individual rights, and when the court is acting to restrict, expand, secure, or protect that justice or those freedoms, we have a different feeling about what is going on than we do in the regular course of judicial process. This, then, is a characteristic of a political trial, good or bad.

CHARACTERISTICS OF GOOD POLITICAL TRIALS

At this point, we can at least partially define a bad political trial in terms of a court's behavior being in some recognizable way repressive of the rights or needs of certain individuals and groups in a context that does not objectively call for such behavior. Consequently, the intent of the court is not concerned with either the advancement of certain principles we hold dear or the pursuit of certain policies we recognize as most desirable. With such a definition, we can begin to see what might constitute a good political trial: A court's behavior recognizably responsive to the rights or needs of various groups or individuals in a context allowing a recognition of such rights or the granting of such needs, and intending the advancement or protection of our principles and the pursuit of our most cherished policies.

However, we can make less extensive substitutions in our formulation of a bad political trial to come up with a good one. For example, we might say that a good political trial can also occur when a court's behavior is repressive and violates certain of our principles or runs counter to our policies, so long as the context in which this behavior occurs objectively calls for some form of repression. This idea is controversial, and well explicated and defended in the next chapter. The point remains, however, that identifying the characteristics of bad political trials has delimited the concept of a good political trial as well.

Given the discussion so far, it is probably not a triviality to point out that any good case is heralded by the massing of legal and historical precedent to bolster an intellectually and morally defensible policy. This is perhaps the most necessary characteristic of good political trials. Sometimes, as in the Brandeis Brief cases, it is the sheer weight of the evidence supporting a change in policy, effectively organized and combined with legal precedent and principle, that marks a good political trial. Sometimes, it is the undeniableness of the wrong in terms of our most fundamental values, brought forth deliberately and with care for the preservation of other values and the exigencies of circumstance, that commends a political trial to our sense of justice. Finally, it is often only the fact that at no other point in our political system might these issues, interests, or needs be considered that resigns us to the fact that a political trial is necessary if we are to do the right thing.

For purposes of illustration, let's compare an intellectually and morally tight argument in the same case with one less attentive to these requisites. The majority position in the *Goldman* case has already been mentioned. Briefly, that argument reduces to the proposition that because "within the military community there is simply not the same [individual] autonomy as there is in the larger civilian community . . . courts must give great deference to the professional judgment of military authorities concerning the relative importance of a particular military interest."[66] Of course, this does not follow, and a liberal sprinkling of the opinion with gestures toward the need for "an effective defense on a moment's notice," and "the necessary habits of discipline . . . unity . . . and obedience to orders . . . with no time for debate or reflection,"[67] are more confusing than helpful, and they make us wonder if Justice Rhenquist is still talking about a yarmulke.

As we pointed out, the case was not really about the relationship between a yarmulke and the military interest. Nor was it about how much autonomy an individual may expect when he or she chooses military life. On the one hand, the case was about power and who has it, and so it was undeniably a political trial. But more importantly, it was political because it was about how much recognition and deference the military must give to one of those fundamental human interests the defense of which is the military's sole justification. What, after all, is a military for? It offends one's aesthetic sense at least to watch the military sanctimoniously condemning one of the concerns advanced to justify its existence and its traditional peculiarities. So while we tolerate a certain necessary diminution of those values while people are in the military, we do not usually accord military authority to the right to decide ultimately the proper degree of diminution.

The *Goldman* decision, then, is not intellectually defensible on the record, nor is it morally defensible given its cavalier attitude toward one of our most cherished and constitutionally protected values. It is also questionable under such precedents as *Chappell v. Wallace* and *Sherbert v. Verner*, and a close reading of these cases, on which the majority opinion depends, does not leave us feeling significantly more comfortable. Justice Brennan's dissent, on the other hand, begins with an examination of precedents and argues that they do not support the court's decision. It then proceeds to demonstrate that neither logic nor data support the court's position, to uncover the position's inconsistency with other sections of the military's own regulations permitting certain exceptions to uniform dress, and to argue that the regulations actually discriminate in favor of Christians. Finally, Justice Brennan contends that when so fundamental a value as religious freedom conflicts with a dress code, uncritical deference to military authority is an abdication of the court's historic responsibility, and he offers a test for determining which should prevail in what circumstances. Even if we at first agree with the majority's conclusion, we must admit that Brennan's position is more historically, intellectually, and morally sound and is more than sufficient to call the conclusion into doubt and require a more deliberate consideration. Had this been the majority opinion, we might have said that *Goldman* was a good political trial.

Concern for Human Dignity

Good political trials amass precedent, logical argument, moral argument, historical insight, and a scrupulous attention to our most cherished principles in order to address what our social and political practice has betrayed as our most fundamental concern for human dignity. This is not a concern for the preservation of an abstract or transcendent principle. It is a practical concern for maximizing as far as practicable each individual's opportunity to realize his or her unique potential. It seeks to "impose no sacrifice or constraint on any citizen by virtue of an argument that the citizen could not accept without abandoning his sense of his equal worth."[68]

This concern for human dignity often takes the form of an argument for equal protection, and beyond this, it harkens back to the idea of all men being created equal. But, of course, we are not all equal and we never can be. In our world, people do not begin life on equal terms, and luck, family, raw skill, intelligence, and all the biases of our cultural history converge and leave us all unique. Nor should we imagine that everyone desires equality. Some people eschew it mightily and feel that the only safe course for them is to have someone else tell them what to do. People of this type enlist in an ideology, a religion, or the military because doing so forfeits the responsibilities that equality implies. Yet their ideal does not include humiliation; they do not want to be treated as though they are valueless. They want to have as much equality as they can stand, and those whom history has put on the bottom want as much equality as they can get.

So, the great problem of our civilization is not the distribution of income, the problems of interracial relations, the problem of sexual equality, crime, nor any of the most current issues, such as homosexual rights. These are derivative; they are descended from our preoccupation with human dignity. Certainly, this concern for human dignity was behind the Supreme Court's discovery of a constitutional right to privacy (not mentioned in the Constitution) by pulling together the First, Fourth, Fifth, Ninth, and Fourteenth Amendment penumbras. Consider, simply, what Justice William Douglas said in *Griswold v. Connecticut*: "We deal with a right to privacy older than the Bill of Rights—older than our political parties, older than our school system. Marriage is a coming together for better or for worse . . . and intimate to the degree of being sacred."[69] In brief, the marriage relationship is among the most dignified of human pursuits and for that reason—for the sake of that human dignity—that relationship is protected against intrusion by the state.

Certainly, the concern for human dignity was behind the decision in *Brown v. Board of Education*, when the Court decided that there was really no such thing as "separate but equal,"[70] and the decision in *Heart of Atlanta Motel v. United States*,[71] upholding the congressional power to prohibit racial segregation in privately owned public accommodations. More recently, the decision in *Bohen v. City of East Chicago*, holding that women are entitled to a working environment free of sexual innuendo,[72] and the decision in *Bazemore v. Friday*, confirming the propriety of hiring quotas wherever it is demonstrated they are necessary, have continued the tradition with this concern.[73]

Without our persistent preoccupation with human dignity, there would not be the bevy of personal rights we consider at least natural if not our birthright, and without this birthright, there could be no good political trials because that is what they are all about. They are about individuals seeking, defining, and learning their rights and powers in changing circumstances, and they are always happening because there is in human nature a strong drive to attain and experience such power. Since, however, we all have this will to personal power, we necessarily conflict with the will of everyone else to be as equal as they can stand. But when all is said, we conclude that we cannot have our dignity if others do not have theirs, and so we put the force of our civilization, through the medium of our courts, behind this idea of treating everybody not only as a means but also always as an end.

Concern for the Disenfranchised

When we think about the way our laws are made and executed, the hopeless inequality among groups and individuals is so apparent. The first principle of legislative justice in our system is that everyone should be represented, at least in a general way, when our laws are made, and that when our laws are carried out, the bureaucrats doing so shall be no respecters of persons but will act diligently on everyone's behalf. Certain people, however, are never represented even generally, and the insensitivity of bureaucrats to the special needs of some groups in our society is adequately documented. Toward the beginning of his first term, President Ronald Reagan said that there were no hungry people in America. Later, he assured us that if there were hungry people it was only because they did not know where to find food. Neither of these statements were true, as a perusal of the data presented in the more popular magazines at that time would document.

It was in such a climate of insensitivity that the Supreme Court held that litigation was a form of political activity. In *NAACP v. Button*, it was the court's opinion that

In the context of NAACP objectives, litigation is not a technique of resolving private differences; it is a means for achieving the lawful objectives of equality of treatment by all government, federal, state, and local, for the members of the Negro community in this country. It is thus a form of political expression. Groups which find themselves unable to achieve their objectives through the ballot frequently turn to the courts. . . . The NAACP is not a conventional political party; but the litigation it assists . . . makes possible the distinctive contribution of a minority group to the ideas and beliefs of our society. For such a group, association for litigation may be the most effective form of political association.[74]

So, there is a special type of litigant in many political trials, and the courts give them special consideration. These litigants are "highly dependent upon the judicial process as a means of pursuing their policy interests, usually because they are temporarily, or even permanently, disadvantaged in terms of their abilities to attain successfully their goals in the electoral process, within the elected political institutions or in the bureaucracy."[75]

This dimension of political trials is not completely occupied by traditional minorities or the historically disadvantaged. An *ad hoc* coalition of conservative Republicans and Democrats, for example, organized and focused on the courts as the only available route for pursuing reapportionment in the late 1950s and early 1960s. The result was *Baker v. Carr*, in which the court ruled that apportionment suits could henceforth be heard by the federal courts.[76]

Appropriating the Oppressor's Language and Acts

One of the most fascinating characteristics of good political trials is that they use the tools of oppression to their own ends. One example of this is the Supreme Court's 1956 decision in *Pennsylvania v. Nelson.*[77] There, "finding a libertarian use for the Smith Act, [then Chief Justice] Warren ruled that, in passing that law, Congress had pre-empted the field of sedition and that states were, therefore, barred from punishing such conduct."[78] Similarly, in *Yates v. United States,*[79] the Court redefined what "organize" meant under the Smith Act and what must be "advocated" to run afoul of its provisions. In the process, the Court opened up and secured constitutional protections for the advocacy of ideas, no matter how unpopular or repugnant. In the first case, the Smith Act was used against itself, and in the second, it was used as a vehicle to affirm and expand First Amendment rights.

This characteristic, however, can work against itself. It can as easily signal a bad political trial as a good one. Most of the bad political trials that we have chronicled and analyzed employed the language of the Bill of Rights to pursue contrary ends. So, we must keep in mind that the concern for human dignity is never far from the heart of a good political trial and that an insensitivity to the impact of a policy on human dignity probably signals a bad political trial.

Some people may have the notion that it is natural for people to welcome change in the furtherance of personal dignity. It is also natural to identify and sympathize with those who are being denied this dignity and to resent those who dehumanize others. This, however, is true only as long as familiar things are happening and the change we experience is not too unexpected. But when circumstances are out of control and we do not know what to do, yet something must be done, it is just as natural for us to begin thinking in terms of "black and white" or "us versus them." That is why it is so easy for facile opportunists to gain political advantage. People are clamoring to be led against an identifiable enemy, and they are impatient with leaders who find this unreasonable.

On the other hand, there may be reasonable leaders in such circumstances who perceive a need to do certain things out of the ordinary, and it is quite a trick to determine exactly what the proper things are. This is the topic of the next chapter, where we will discuss the kinds of things that are justifiable in political trials in different social contexts.

NOTES

1. See E. O. Kirchheimer, *Political Justice: The Use of Legal Procedure for Political Ends* (Princeton, NJ: Princeton University Press, 1961), 6. See also T. L. Becker, ed., *Political Trials* (Indianapolis, IN: Bobbs-Merrill, 1971), xii–xiii.

2. A. I. Solzhenitsyn, *The Gulag Archipegalo*, vol. 1 (New York: Harper and Row, 1973), 306–309.

3. *Martin v. Struthers*, 319 U.S. 141 (1943); *Cohens v. Virginia*, 788 F2 247 (1964); *McGowan v. Maryland*, 366 U.S. 420 (1961).

4. See E. G. McCloskey, *The American Supreme Court* (Chicago: University of Chicago Press, 1960), 26–80.

5. Ibid.

6. 5 U.S. (1 Cranch) 137 (1803).

7. 7 Wall. 506; 19 L.Ed. 264 (1869).

8. See D. Berrigan, *The Trial of the Catonsville 9* (Boston: Beacon Press, 1970).

9. *Marbury v. Madison*, 1 Cranch 137 (1803).

10. *California Reporter* (Appendix), 1965.

11. Louis Hartz, *The Liberal Tradition in America* (New York: Harcourt, Brace and World, Inc., 1955), 6, 11.

12. See E. O. Wright, *The Politics of Punishment* (New York: Harper and Colophon Books, 1973), 3–21, for examples and a more detailed analysis.

13. See Berrigan, *The Trial of the Catonsville 9*.

14. See R. Florence, *Fritz: The Story of a Political Assassin* (New York: Daily Press, 1971).

15. 347 U.S. 254, 90 S.Ct. 1011, 25 L.E.D. 2d 287 (1970).

16. See *Convention on the Prevention and Punishment of the Crime of Genocide*, December 9, 1948, 78 U.N.T.S. 277: Arts 1–4 (Basic Documents 3.2); *International Convention on the Elimination of All Forms of Racial Discrimination* March 7, 1966, 660 U.N.T.S. 195 Reprinted in 5 I.L.M. 352 (1966); Arts 1–3, 5, 6, (Basic Documents 3.11); and *Universal Declaration of Human Rights* Dec. 10, 1948, U.N.G.A. Res. 217(III), U.N. Doc. A/810, at 71 (1948): Arts 1–3, 5–11, 17, 19–21, 23, 24, 28–30 (Basic Documents 3.3).

17. R. M. Belknap, *Cold War Political Justice* (Westport, CT: Greenwood Press, 1977), 137.

18. Ibid.

19. U. D. Volkan, "The Need to Have Enemies & Allies: A Developmental Approach," 6 *Political Psychology* 224 (June 1985).

20. H. F. Stein, "Psychological Complementarity in Soviet-American Relations," 6 *Political Psychology* 252–254 (June 1985).

21. Ibid.

22. *Dennis v. U.S.*, 341 U.S. 494 (1951).

23. *Schenck v. U.S.*, 249 U.S. 47 (1919); *Frohwerk v. U.S.*, 249 U.S. 204 (1919); and *Debs v. U.S.*, 249 U.S. 284 (1919).

24. A. Hoffman, *The Trial of the Chicago Seven* (New York: Dial Press, 1970).

25. Ibid.

26. Belknap, *Political Justice*, 161.

27. *Dennis v. U.S.*, 341 U.S. 404 (1951); *Schenck v. U.S.*, 249 U.S. 49 (1919); *U.S. v. Spock* (1972).

28. W. Gellhorn, (Ed.), *The States and Subversion* (New York: Cornell University Press, 1976), 377–382.

29. *U.S. v. Snepp*, 444 U.S. at 512–513, (1979).

30. Slip Opinion No. 84–1097, March 25, 1986.

31. Andrew Kull, *The Color Blind Constitution* (Boston: Harvard University Press, 1992).

32. M. Deutch, "Conflict Resolution: Theory and Practice," 4 *Political Psychology* 3 (1983).

33. *U.S. v. Schenck*, 249 U.S. 52 (1919).

34. *Frohwerk v. U.S.*, 249 U.S. 209 (1919).

35. *Dennis v. U.S.*, 341 U.S. 511 (1951).

36. 98 U.S. 145 (1879).

37. Ibid., 148.

38. M. Blain, "The Role of Death in Political Conflict," 63 *Psychoanalytical Review*, 250–265 (1976).

39. *Schenck v. U.S.*, 249 U.S. 52 (1919).

40. 467 F. Supp. 990 (W.D. Wis.), appeal dismissed 610 F.2d 819 (7th Cir., 1979).

41. *U.S. v. The Progressive*, 467 F. Supp. 995.

42. 310 U.S. 586.

43. *West Virginia State Board of Education v. Barnette*, 319 U.S. 624 (1943).

44. "Ruling on Yarmulke Upheld by Court," The *New York Times*, March 26, 1986, 13.

45. *Prince v. Massachusetts*, 321 U.S. 158 (1944).

46. 230 U.S. 616.

47. Ibid.

48. 247 U.S. 357 (1927).

49. 137 U.S. 333 (1890).

50. Gellhorn, ed., *The Strategy and Subversion*, 359–360.

51. 341 U.S. 494 (1951).

52. Belknap, *Cold War Political Justice*.

53. On each of these points see *Delli Pauli v. U.S.*, 352 U.S. 232 (1957); *Pinkerton v. U.S.*, 328 U.S. 640 (1946); *U.S. v. Schneidernman*, 106 F.Supp. 906; *Glasser v. U.S.*, 315 U.S. 65 (1942); A. S. Goldstein, "Conspiracy to Defraud the United States," 68 *Yale L.J.* 404 (1959).

54. See R. A. Sealer, "The Dombrowski Suit as an Effective Weapon for Social Change: Reflections from Without and Within," 18 *Kansas L.R.* 237 (1970), especially Part III.

55. J. Mitford, *The Trial of Doctor Spock* (New York: Knopf, 1969), 5.

56. *U.S. v. Snepp*, 456 F.Supp. 176 (Ed. Va. 1978).

57. *U.S. v. Snepp*, 595 F.2d 926 (4th Cir., 1979).

58. *Snepp v. U.S.*, 444 U.S. 507 (1980).

59. Ibid. at 511, note 6.

60. 376 U.S. 254 (1964).

61. Ibid., 273.

62. *New York Times v. U.S.*, 403 U.S. 713 (1971).

63. Ibid., 724.

64. R. Ferrari, "Political Crime," 20 *Columbia L.R.* 308 (1920).

65. Ibid.

66. *Goldman v. Weinburger*, 546 F2d 477 (1972).

67. Ibid.

68. R. Dworkin, *A Matter of Principle* (Boston: Harvard University Press, 1985), 205.

69. 381 U.S. 479 (1965).

70. 347 U.S. 483 (1954).

71. 379 U.S. 241 (1968).

72. 799 F2d 476 (1988).

73. 848 F2 476 (1989).

74. 371 U.S. 415 (1963).

75. R. C. Cortner, "Strategies & Tactics of Litigants in Constitutional Cases," 27 *Journal of Public Law* 287 (1971).

76. 364 U.S. 898 (1960).

77. 350 U.S. 497 (1956).

78. Belknap, *Cold War Political Justice*, 240.

79. 354 U.S. 298 (1957).

Chapter Four

Justifying Political Trials

In our civilization, where people deliberately change their institutions from day-to-day in courts, legislatures, and administrative agencies, we need some practical way of taking our bearings and employing our courts appropriately toward necessary ends. We need a coherent and realistic framework to help us decide what to do and how to go about doing it. The purpose of this chapter is to show how we might determine what is happening around us so that we can properly evaluate the political trials that are occurring and cope with our civilization by using the right kind of political trial at the right time.

We have shown that our political and legal situation is a reflection of our social experience. That experience is the basis for deciding what trials are political and which political trials are justified. To do this, we suggest a framework for comparing these experiences as offered by Philip Nonet and Philip Selznick in their book *Law and Society in Transition: Toward Responsive Law.*[1] Nonet and Selznick suggest that the varieties of political, economic, and social experience (i.e., a civilization's "form of life") result in a legal system with three "characteristic postures:"

1. repressive (the legal system is the servant of a repressive power)
2. autonomous (the legal system is a differentiated institution capable of taming repression and protecting its own integrity)
3. responsive (the legal system acts as a facilitator in response to social needs and aspirations)

These labels are not intended to describe empirically or logically distinct types of systems. All legal systems are mixed, incorporating aspects of all three. The labels are meant to describe postures struck by a society in response to its ongoing experience. The society adopts one or another posture at any given time depending on how well each then works to more efficiently circulate power in order to get things done.

For our purposes, we argue that each of these postures is justifiable given a proper social context. Each is a mode of action available through the courts in trying to effectively employ power to produce action and attain results. Its legitimacy derives from how well it functions to energize and direct the exercise of power at any given time, and it develops from the circulation through the courts of the prevailing social discourse. In other words, the courts act as places of collective negotiation over the proper distribution and employment of power and provide institutionalized procedures for deciding which of these postures will be struck. Consequently, what constitutes a political trial and what constitutes its justification depend on (1) which posture is being struck, and (2) how justified that posture is given the prevailing mix of social, economic, and political experiences.

Moreover, we infer from Nonet and Selznick that repressive law is justified and repressive trials are seen as nonpolitical, when societies experience widespread and deep disorganization and unrest in the face of urgent tasks and scarce resources.[2] Similarly, autonomous law is justified, and trials that define and reinforce given social, political, and economic prerogatives, while ensuring that no one goes beyond his or her appointed spheres, are seen as nonpolitical, when order is not enough and there is a need for stability, legitimacy, and the taming of repression.[3] Finally, responsive law is justified, and trials addressing the broadest range of political, economic, and social problems in an attempt to strike proper and fluid balances of interests are seen as nonpolitical, when the stability and resources of a society present no problems, the most urgent of tasks are met, and society becomes concerned with expanding the rights and privileges of people with a view toward facilitating and promoting the good life.[4]

With this as our foundation, it is a small step to argue that as a stable and mature society blessed with vast resources, we strike a stance at the autonomous-to-responsive end of the spectrum and recognize as political only political trials from our more repressive eras. We recognize them as unjust because we are evaluating them from the social, economic, and political experiences that make an autonomous-to-responsive posture possible. At the same time, because our stance is autonomous-to-responsive, we are ambiguous about trials involving such issues as consumer rights, civil rights, the rights of the elderly, the rights of children, women's rights, privacy rights, the rights of patients, the rights of the incompetent, environmental rights, and (on the international level) human rights.

All such trials are, of course, directly aimed at redistributing power in our society and indirectly aimed at shifting the benefits and burdens of social living, but we often consider them nonpolitical, doing what courts are supposed to be doing when they act responsively. On the other hand, there is a spreading feeling that courts often go too far in these areas and so should restrict themselves to more traditional (i.e., less political) activities. This reflects changing political, economic, and social experiences, causing us to rethink what is justified and what is not and so redefining what we call a political trial.

To substantiate our argument, we must demonstrate each of these points. To begin, however, we should first say a word about justice. Justice is the key concept in each step of our argument, and what we mean by that term is critical to our point. To define justice is essential for knowing why different kinds of political trials are justified at different times.

JUSTICE, POLITICS, AND LAW

It is generally understood that the dividing up of power and wealth in our society and the deciding of what constitutes a good human being goes on everyday in our civil and criminal courts. In every court, each of us has his or her legally appointed share of goals, rights, duties, and responsibilities rearranged constantly and incrementally, and each of us is criticized or extolled, however tacitly, for his or her behavior.

What should our shares be? What is not a good way to be a human being? What are the limits of our rights and responsibilities? In brief, what constitutes a just distribution? These issues are not settled, and if we think they will settle themselves, others will settle them for us. If we do not wrestle with these issues, we cannot complain too loudly about the outcome because we have not met our responsibilities as citizens to choose among alternatives and stand for what we have chosen. Equally important, if courts do not wrestle and choose they cannot be confident that a particular decision, and the redistributions it works, is just.

But how can courts choose? They need a coherent but not rigid idea of justice. Rigid ideas of justice simply do not produce satisfactory choices. Aristotle, for example, thought we should distribute according to the principles of merit and equality but since he was an aristocrat with a low opinion of labor and non-Greeks, he forgot the poor and the oppressed, neither of whom he felt were either equal or meritorious. Marx and some French socialists, on the other hand, suggested that we give to each according to his or her needs, but needs proved an elusive and ever-expanding yardstick. Adam Smith suggested, "To each according to what he can demand for what he produces." But this produced boom and bust cycles and a series of court decisions during our own Great Depression that consistently frustrated every attempt of the legislative and executive branches to set us back on the economically productive and socially stable course. Kinder people have suggested distributions to each according to what they need for the development of their unique capacities, while others have said that we must first work out a distribution that keeps our society and economic system functioning to produce the greatest good for the greatest number. This would then allow all of these other ends to be pursued.

Each of these ideas has merit. So, a court might reasonably conclude that producing a just decision involves balancing merit, equality, need, liberty, and utility in the different contexts identified by Nonet and Selznick. But this is not the problem; it is simply impossible. We cannot settle on any particular criterion of justice without oppressing someone. Moreover, each of these ideas remains an integral part of our ongoing social discourse, each is championed by individuals and groups for which it is an important tool in their tactics and techniques for gaining, retaining, and utilizing power, and each has been to some extent accepted in different contexts as facilitating the circulation of power within our system. Thus, our concept of justice in this society is so intricate that stressing any one of these ideas to the exclusion of others is probably unjust in terms of our culture, history, and tradition. Only through the simultaneous and balanced pursuit of each, might we obtain some optimum among them and approximate as a society what we mean by justice.

What constitutes a balanced pursuit is context dependent, and that is what we must decide, case by case, for each of Nonet and Selznick's categories. Therefore, we will take each of Nonet and Selznick's legal systems, and examine them in context until we have a good idea of which type of law and court behavior is justified in which sort of context.

REPRESSIVE LAW, POLITICAL TRIALS, AND JUSTICE

Political oppression is not foreign to America. Blacks, women, Japanese Americans during the Second World War, socialists at the turn of the century, Communists during the 1950s, drinkers during the 1920s, and social reformers and war protestors during the 1960s are only several of innumerable groups whose human rights, privileges, and immunities have been denied by the direct action of our executives, legislatures, and courts. Sometimes the courts have been used to legitimate the oppression, but at other times, they have initiated it. So the question is not whether our courts have or will oppress people in America but when (if ever) such repression is just and when (if ever) oppression might make a society a better place to live.

Let's begin with the simplest situation: an emerging nation. Among these people, there is often no ongoing nor shared political form of life. There is not that supporting context of shared political practices and beliefs that leaders require to fulfill their responsibilities. So there is a poverty of political resources and a set of urgent tasks facing the government. A supporting political context must be created, this is the function of oppression. Here, we might say that the need for the creation of a nation and the utility of oppression in meeting this need are weightier than both the individual liberties and the equal treatment of groups.

We must, however, be careful. We do not mean to say that the task of nation building justifies any form of oppression. It is one thing to control the press, deny universal suffrage, promote the interests of one class over another, and direct the economy. It is another to massacre your opponents, their families, their pets, and their sympathizers. Despite the prejudices we may have developed in our constitutional democracy, it is possible to oppress in ways that do a minimum amount of damage to human dignity and recognize the integrity of human beings. So the potential for evil lies not in what is done but how we go about doing it.

A good example of this occurred in the United States following the Declaration of Independence. In Pennsylvania, the newly created state constitution faced opposition from nearly everyone, including conservative Whigs who tried to prevent its execution, pacifist members of various religious sects, and loyalist supporters of the king. This was an untenable situation given the recent war, the general unfamiliarity with independence, and the natural tendency of people in fluid and rapidly changing circumstances to have second thoughts. To prod a reluctant citizenry into supporting the newly created state, Pennsylvania required loyalty oaths from voters and office holders. Failure to comply led to a denial of political rights and some economic chastisement—but not to execution, the more traditional approach to treason.

The threat of execution was used, under the Treason Act of 1777, for those who failed to pay allegiance to the state and were guilty of levying war against Pennsylvania. The point of this law was not to execute anyone nor to root out traitors. There were just too many difficult citizens in important political, social, and economic positions in the structure of colonial Pennsylvania. The idea, rather, was to encourage neutrals, die-hard loyalties, and formerly prominent citizens to at least acquiesce. The procedure was simple: First the most prominent diehards were identified and accused by a bill of attainder. Then, they swore a loyalty oath and the interests of the state were served by a dismissal of the charges.

All in all, this system worked pretty well: of 113 conditionally attained, 45 were presented to the grand jury, 22 were indicted, 17 stood trial, and 2 were executed. More importantly, the example of those prosecuted served to quiet things down until the new nation had a chance to breathe. While many people suffered what would be intolerable political and economic sanctions under any other circumstance, there was most often a certain discipline applied, keeping the undeniable oppression within acceptable and generally humane limits.

Of course, the need for repressive law is not limited to nascent states. As Nonet and Selznick point out, even where a stable form of government exists, "a highly rational and liberal minded administrator may have to fall back on repressive force if there is no other means to maintaining public order."[5] One good example of this in American history is Abraham Lincoln's suspension of the writ of habeas corpus and his ordered summary arrest and detention of all those suspected of engaging in, or about to engage in, disloyal acts during the Civil War. As many as 25,000 arrests were made, but most were never tried; they were released after swearing loyalty oaths.

The problem, of course, is to distinguish real threats to the nation's integrity and the sovereignty of its people from legitimate difference and protest, which may (under appropriate circumstances) be a citizen's civic duty. John Rawls is helpful here. In *A Theory of Justice*, he calls such protest civil disobedience and distinguishes it from a threat to the nation by pointing out that it is an act addressed to those holding political power, the purpose of which is to preserve the Constitution and our political institutions from what is understood to be a threat from those holding positions of authority.[6] As Rawls indicates, "Civil disobedience . . . is one of the stabilizing devices of a constitutional system, although by definition an illegal one. . . . By re-ricting injnrtion within the limitr of fidolity to lnw, it rnrvor to inhibit du partures from justice and to correct them when they occur."[7] Seen in this light, it is court action against those engaged in civil disobedience that threatens not only the rights and interests of protestors but the constitutional system itself. Clearly, that sort of political trial cannot be justified by balancing national need and considerations of utility against liberty and equality. The court becomes part of the threat it is supposed to defend us against if its engagement in a political trial is to be justifiable.

This argument, of course, makes certain important assumptions. First, it assumes that those being disobedient have honestly sought appropriate objects of civil disobedience, and that this is clear or should be clear to the police and public officials:

If one views such disobedience as a political act addressed to the justice of the community, then it seems reasonable . . . to limit it to instances of substantial and clear injustices.[8]

Second, it assumes that the normal legal means of redress have failed and that all reasonable options have been exhausted. Finally, the argument assumes that the civil disobedience does not threaten the ultimate integrity of the state. The disobedience must be such that it will not lead to a breakdown of legitimate authority (though it may affect those in authority), nor a breakdown in the ability of political institutions to respond to and deal with the situation in a manner beneficial to everyone. Given these constraints, however, it does seem that civil disobedience is a legitimate and, at times, necessary form of political participation. Its punishment by the courts is then recognizably political and recognizably unjust.

Of course, this is a far cry from the clearly unjustified political kidnappings, bombings, and assassinations that have periodically broken out all over Europe, South America, and the Middle East during the 1970s and 1980s. Nevertheless, one hopeful note persists. Despite all the political terrorism, western European countries have managed to keep human dignity and democratic ideals clearly in mind as they take the necessary steps toward keeping the public peace. We must also remember that Rawls is writing in a stable and mature political context in which the government has the means, expertise, time, and political resources to be responsive to a widening number of individual and group concerns. But there are moments in the history of many countries when war, natural disaster, economic failure, or social revolution can make such tolerance impossible. The trick is to know when this is so or when disasters are being used as excuses to be intolerant. We need to look at some recognizably bad political trials to get an idea of what to look for.

In the European context, a political trial that was obviously repressive and unjust was that of Anne Boleyn. She was accused of adultery and incest by England's Henry VIII, who desired a male heir, which Anne failed to produce, and who had become enamored of Anne's maid as a promising source of such an heir. The court at Westminster obliged him, tried Anne, found her guilty, sentenced her to death, and executed her. Henry married the maid, and his daughter by Anne eventually became queen. This was certainly an instance in which it was expedient for the executive to use the courts for the satisfaction of personal ends, regardless of the human rights and dignity of others. So, it was oppressive and clearly unjust. Anne did not deserve the outcome nor did the trial serve any national need. There is nothing to balance against Anne's loss of liberty and inequitable treatment before the courts, and we can only find some justice in that Henry came to a miserable end.

A case closer to being justified but still clearly unjust was that of Sir Thomas More. More was caught in the middle of a struggle for power between the English church and state. Refusing to articulate an assent to Henry VIII's Royal Declaration of State Supremacy, More was charged with treason. He was tried and executed, but only after the Crown's prosecutor, Archbishop Thomas Cromwell, fairly pleaded with More to assent and provided him with more than one rationale for reconciling his conscience with the needs of the Crown.[9]

The issue of justice here turns on the need of the state to get More's assent at the price of either his freedom of conscience or of his life. How dire was the state's need? How important was it that More assent? Was the ultimate integrity of the state threatened? Had all reasonable options been exhausted? The record seems to indicate that the state's need was not dire and that Henry simply went into a rage over the machinations of Pope Paul III, setting in motion a sequence of events precluding more reasonable options and leading to More's execution. The Crown simply used the courts in an attempt to effectuate a policy, and when that failed, it used the courts to eliminate a dissenter.

Joan of Arc and Galileo experienced similar problems. Both of their trials were attempts by the Catholic church to maintain its authority over Joan's voices and Galileo's science.[10] But such uses of the courts are not restricted to either a nation's executive or the leaders of powerful political groups, such as the church. There are times when the entire population of a country exhibits a certain hysteria that strikes responsive chords in the courts. The trials of Dreyfus, Sacco and Vanzetti, and the Rosenbergs to some extent illustrate this hysteria in the United States. Regardless of whether the particular individuals charged were guilty or innocent, an examination of the history of these trials supports the idea that the courts became the tools of a vengeful or frightened public, lost their objectivity, and repressed individuals who had often become more symbols of an intangible threat than actual dangers in themselves.

These trials give us some idea of how to recognize bad, repressive political trials. Of course, our thesis is that all repressive uses of the courts are not unjustified. We need to provide some examples supportive of our thesis to compare with the cases just discussed and to show that once the balance is properly struck and the state's needs are clear and stringent, repressive political trials can be just and the duty of those in government.

Perhaps the most outstanding examples of justifiable repression used by the courts are those of Socrates and Christ. Socrates was actively spreading dissension and undermining a tenuous democracy established as part of the Athenian postwar reconstruction. The Pelloponnesian War had been disastrous socially, politically, and economically. The extremity of the need, the urgent tasks facing the government, the poverty of available resources and the collapse of what had once been a supporting context of institutions created a crisis situation. Moreover, Socrates was aware of all this and so in some sense must have understood the possible consequences (in fact his prosecutor tried at length to gain his assent to the new democracy much as in the case of Sir Thomas More). There is, in other words, evidence that he deserved some rebuke.

Much of the same analysis can be applied to Christ. Both Rome and the Sanhedrin understood Christ's theology as revolutionary. It was a direct threat to the precariously balanced relationship between the Roman governors and the Jewish leadership. The context was violent. Judea was occupied, extremist groups (e.g., the Zealots and the Essenes) were showing an inclination toward religious terrorism, and Christ had violently attacked merchants and bankers in the Temple of Jerusalem. Worse, mobs were forming and proclaiming Christ King of Israel.[11] As with Socrates, Christ cannot be said to have been ignorant of these events.

So, we cannot complain too convincingly about repression in either case. There are real arguments that it was necessary. What we might complain about is the quality of the repression. There might have been options other than death available to make the point clear (though it does seem that in the case of Christ, at least, other things were tried). A more modern example illustrates some other options.

In *The Queen v. Dudley and Stephens*,[12] four shipwrecked sailors, afloat in a raft, starved for twenty-five days before killing and eating one among them who had been unconscious for some time. They were charged with murder. The court found "that if the men had not fed upon the body of the boy then would probably not have survived," and that "the boy, being in a much weaker condition, was likely to have died before the others."[13] Still, the court found the sailors guilty and sentenced them to death.

The political problem here is obvious. One the one hand, none of the sailors deserved what happened to them. The extremity of the need was patent and the utility of the remedy used was undeniable. There was even an attempt to be equitable. Instead of reverting to brute strength to decide the issue, the conscious sailors discussed their options for several days and the relative merits of who should die. They then delayed implementing their decision in the hopes that a rescue vessel would show up. So justice would seem to argue in their favor; finding them guilty and sentencing them to death would seem oppressive.

On the other hand, an acquittal or drastic reduction of the charge would send a dangerous signal. It would suggest that in order to save your own life you may lawfully take that of another who is neither threatening you nor guilty of any illegal act whatsoever. The high seas were dangerous enough at that time without the acceptance of this idea. Besides, this practice could be used on land as well. So, the government, understandably uncomfortable with the social implications of doing strict justice to the individuals, struck upon a plan. The court found the defendants guilty of the maximum offense and imposed the maximum penalty. This sent the proper signals. Then the Crown commuted their sentences to six months in prison. Together, the courts and the Crown worked out the best justice they could manage in the situation. The sailors were oppressed but their dignity and integrity were preserved to a practical extent in the face of social need.

Perhaps in the cases of Socrates and Christ, each could have been loudly pronounced guilty, solemnly sentenced to death, sadly sent to prison to await execution, and then unceremoniously bounced out of the country on one pretext or another after things had calmed down. In fact, any popular history of the trial of Socrates indicates that the Athenian authorities and the population expected Socrates to leave town after being charged, and no steps were taken to prevent this eventuality. Charging Socrates was a political symbol, and Socrates stayed for his own purposes. Once again, it is the quality and not the fact of oppression that we must quarrel with in such situations. But we now turn to one problem with oppressive political trials even when that oppression is warranted.

We have assumed in the discussion so far that the citizens ruled by the government seeking to preserve itself were neither widely nor intensely opposed to that government or that the government either shared their values, was sympathetic to their welfare, was interested in promoting their growth and development, had developed from or was not threatening to their "form of life," or let the citizens mostly alone to pursue their welfare in traditional ways. In brief, we assumed that the oppressing government was treating the citizens as ends and not just as means. In emerging nations, for example, we argued that oppression was justifiable. The assumption was that many of these nations were developing from tribal cultures without the traditions of pluralism and democracy that we find in the West. Similarly, while Rome certainly occupied Israel by force at the time of Christ, it left the institutions and traditions of Israel largely intact. On the other hand, there are situations in which this is not the case. In such nations, the justification for repression based on necessity is much less convincing.

South Africa is perhaps the most prominent example. There is no pretext in that country that the government is treating its people as ends and not means. The laws of apartheid secure separate "forms of life" for blacks and whites and ensure the dominance of whites. Broadly speaking, only white people vote, make laws, and work in the courts. In such a case, although the government may need repressive political trials to survive, we cannot say they are justified as we have argued above. Courts are not being used to create a supporting context nor to secure a weakened or immature structure of socially developed institutions in times of urgent need. They are being used to subjugate. They give no opportunity for a context or structure of institutions to develop out of the country's "form of life," which work to dignity the country's citizens. Rather, they impose an alien structure contrary to the interests of the general population.

AUTONOMOUS LAW, POLITICS, AND JUSTICE

At some point, repression needs taming or becomes unnecessary, and people aspire to "a government of laws and not of men." Young nations must build on the accomplishments of repressive law by gaining a legitimacy based on something other than force, and the accomplishments must take root among the people as the right or comparatively best form of government. Similarly, a mature nation having experienced rapid change or crisis needs to retrench, regain lost legitimacy, and set out again on the proper bearings. These are the functions and ends of an autonomous legal system, and political trials calculated to ensure these ends are clearly justifiable and probably not considered political by the people or the government.

One reason autonomous legal systems are legitimate is that they acquire sufficient independent authority to apply the law to leaders as well as followers. In exchange for this authority, they agree to stay out of policy making as much as possible. This is how autonomous law remains a mechanism of social control; it remains committed to the policy it receives from the political community and applies the rules strictly to the people and the government. It is a connecting link between these two great divisions of society, but it is ultimately committed to legitimizing the government, diffusing dissent by mediation and adjudication on a case-by-case basis, and "depoliticizing" issues that might otherwise explode. Autonomous law functions as a political force to (1) control government officials, (2) control the people, (3) legitimize the government, and (4) dampen dissent.

People under an autonomous system would probably have no trouble recognizing as political the trials we have just examined under repressive systems. In an autonomous legal system, courts, congresses, and executives are supposed to be distinct. The use of the courts by any of the latter is obviously and decidedly unjust. In addition, it would be clear when the law's sphere of influence was being invaded. Also, it would be obvious when people used, to their own political advantage, certain technical violations of the laws by their opponents. In each of these cases, the people could understand such political trials as unjust since none of the four political functions of an autonomous system were being met. In this way, people under an autonomous system understand that what seems to be a political trial is unjust. Let's take a look at some examples.

Probably the clearest examples of just political trials that do not seem political for those under autonomous systems occur when regimes (the king and his advisors, elected executives and their "inner circle") are tried. For those operating under autonomous systems, the values and legitimacy of stabilized and mature governments are properly challenged through the legal system when they do not stay in their proper spheres and behave like repressive systems when managing their crises.

Autonomous systems would declare the trial of England's Charles I just and nonpolitical, since he was charged with "levying war against the Parliament and the Kingdom" when he used English courts to oppress his enemies. Louis XVI of France did the same thing and was similarly charged with waging war against the people, so his trial, too, would be considered just and nonpolitical.[14] At the same time, however, the trials prosecuted by Charles and Louis to secure the legitimacy of their own regimes would be understood as political and unjust, as would the trials which were prosecuted under Pennsylvania's law requiring loyalty oaths and Lincoln's proclamation establishing summary arrests and detentions. Being safely distant from the form of life and social experiences engendering these repressive trials, people under autonomous systems see little in them that might justify even a measured oppression toward a necessary governmental end.

Still, people under autonomous systems have problems justifying the trial of regimes, even in the cases just mentioned. The trial has a legitimacy problem under their own rationale. By what authority does a court try a government? One the one hand, if courts are a branch of government, their legitimacy and values must be in question too. Alternately, if courts are separate from the other branches, where do they get their power?

There are two possibilities: Courts in autonomous systems may claim guardianship of a fundamental and "higher law," or they may claim to be guarantor of the popular will. Indeed, trials of regimes are often battles between these two ideals, and if the court claims one as the basis of its prosecution, the defendant argues the other as the basis of its defense. Interestingly, trials of regimes under autonomous systems are usually most successful when courts call on the popular will, since that usually has the greatest legitimizing effect.

In the trial of Charles I, for example, the Lord President Bradshaw told Charles:

As that law is your superior, so truly sir, there is something that is superior to the law, and that is indeed the present or author of the law, and that is the people of England.[15]

Charles, in turn, told the court:

Remember, I am your king, your lawful king, and what sins you bring upon your heads, and the judgment of God upon this land; think well upon it, I say, think well upon it, before you go further from one sin to a greater . . . I shall not betray my trust: I have a trust committed to me by God, by old and lawful descent; I will not betray it, to answer to a new and unlawful authority.[16]

So, the will of the people was arrayed against the will of God, and Charles was beheaded.

In the case of political repression, American history reveals no dearth of trials regarding the abuses of power by the executive and legislative branches. Watergate, Abscam, and the Iran-Contra affair are the more sensational instances that come to mind. In Watergate, President Nixon used his position to subvert the normal processes of the two-party system by ordering the burglarizing of the Democratic National headquarters. In Abscam, congressmen used their positions to subvert the normal processes of policy making by taking bribes, and in the Iran-Contra affair, President Reagan used his position to subvert the congressional will by trading with terrorists and using the resulting funds to support a group of subversives in Nicaragua. Under an autonomous approach, the resulting trials would serve as political even though they served each of the political functions that courts have within that system. During the Watergate scandal, for example, Judge

John Sirica became *Time* magazine's "Man of the Year" for upholding the idea that public officials are controlled by law, thereby helping to legitimize a system of government facing a constitutional crisis and a crisis of confidence within the American public. Similarly, in the Abscam prosecutions, even though some were concerned that the FBI investigations seemed to focus exclusively on liberal Democrats in Congress, no objection was raised, since those involved had clearly violated a public trust. Officials were controlled, dissent was dampened, and the government was legitimized.

The exercise of law in an autonomous system is meant to control citizens as well as officials, and there are many trials in American history chronicling the temptation to violence as a result of popular frustration. Probably the clearest case of this sort was the trial of Karl Armstrong for bombing the Army Math Resource Center at the University of Wisconsin in 1970. The bombing accidentally killed one person and injured five others.

Armstrong's defense argued that he turned to violence only after his experience at the 1968 Democratic Convention convinced him that neither working within the system nor peacefully demonstrating would stop the Vietnam War. So Armstrong's act was one of civil disobedience, morally justified by the unresponsiveness of those in power and their fundamentally illegal and immoral acts. The prosecution naturally did not stress the motivation (the conduct of war and its propriety is not within the judicial sphere), but the act (violence clearly violated the rules of the game).[17] The defense was unsuccessful because in this sort of situation it is unconvincing to argue that Armstrong's prosecution was a political trial. Deadly violence in all but repressive systems is such a breach of the rules that the political motivations of the defendant and the government are irrelevant. Of course, the political function of courts in controlling people with this sort of violent tendency toward government is considered nonpolitical and just.

But the trial of the "Catonsville Nine" for burning the records of a local draft board was something else. As in the Armstrong case, it occurred just as the civil rights movement and the antiwar movement were taking violent turns. The fundamental legitimacy of the state was being questioned in the streets, in congress, and on campuses. Moreover, the economy, though superficially booming, was strained by the demands of the war on poverty and the war in Vietnam. In short, it occurred when the government was in crisis. So when the Berrigan brothers raided the Catonsville Selective Service offices and burned the draft records, the prosecutor predictably argued the irrelevancy of the war's morality:

I want it clearly understood that the government is not about to put itself in the position—has not heretofore and is not now—of conducting its policies at the end of a string tied to the consciences of these nine defendants. This trial does not include the issues of the Vietnam conflict. It does not include the issue of whether the United States ought to be in the conflict or out of it.

The government quite candidly admits that the position these defendants took is reasonable—as to the fact that the war is illegal, that it is immoral, that it is against religious principles, that any reasonable man could take that view. . . . But this prosecution is the government's response, the law's response, the people's response, to what the defendants did.[18]

The defense, however, cast the act as one of legitimate and justified civil disobedience:

It is not a question of records which are independent of life. We are not talking about driving licenses or licenses to operate a brewery. We are speaking of one kind of records. No others so directly affect life and death on a mass scale, as do these. They affect every mother's son who is registered with any Board. These records stand quite literally for life and death to young men.

The defendants did not go to Catonsville to act as criminals, to frighten Mrs. Murphy, or to annoy or hinder her. They were there to complete a symbolic act (first of all) which we claim is a free speech act. And secondly, they were there to impede and interfere with the operation of a system which they have concluded (and it is not an unreasonable belief as the government has told you) is immoral, illegal, and is destroying innocent people around the world.[19]

The Berrigans were certainly addressing their act to those in power, and they were honestly guided by the idea of preserving some fundamental values we hold dear. Apparently, this was clear to public officials (as the prosecutor's statement reveals), and the record shows that some attempts were made to employ normal means of legal redress before and after the Berrigan incident.[20] But the courts considered the involvement in Vietnam a political question outside their proper sphere, and the executive continued to prosecute the war despite heavy congressional and public opposition. Arguably, then, the Berrigan act was a legitimate protest, and reasonable people might conclude that under the circumstances it was a civic duty. The trick is to decide how justified the government was in holding the Berrigans strictly to the rule; and this depends on how far protest in general had gotten out of hand.

We are suggesting that, given the volatility of the situation at that time and the recurring acts of widespread and massive violence (by citizens and police), the Berrigans might justly be held more strictly accountable for their civil disobedience than under calmer circumstances. Although their act probably did not threaten a breakdown of legitimate authority, it was prosecuted in a crisis context. The government may have needed a way of re-establishing control over the populace and dampening dissent without further eroding its legitimacy and an autonomous stance is exactly suited to these ends. Autonomous law controls without oppressing and thereby legitimates the government and lessens dissent. So while the trial of the "Catonsville Nine" was certainly political, it may have been just. It was at least a borderline case.

For an example of unjustly using an autonomous approach for political purposes, consider the prosecution of a county commissioner for the theft of services during his tenure as county coroner.[21] The prosecution took place in Pittsburgh, Pennsylvania, and the commissioner involved coincidentally occupied the county Democratic Party chair. The district attorney was Republican and running for the State Supreme Court. The commissioner had well-known enemies within his own party who helped initiate and pursue the prosecution while using it to force his resignation as party chair.

As it turned out, the commissioner technically stole $115,000 worth of county services by bringing tissue specimens from his private lab to the county lab for pathology and toxicology testing. But "the work done was part of an educational program for pathology residents studying at the morgue; his private lab performed free tests for the county on a reciprocal basis; and the private work was never done to the detriment of public work."[22] The law was thus technically violated but not substantively violated, and although he was acquitted by a jury, the technical violation was used successfully to attain desired political ends (his removal as party chair and publicity for the district attorney running for the bench). Here the proper political goal of keeping public officials in line was not the point and the prosecution is therefore recognizably political and unjust.

What cannot be considered as political trials under an autonomous system are the day-to-day enforcements of political, social, and economic advantages and disadvantages structured into the system of rules that the courts are enforcing. Rules and the spheres of influence they delineate guarantee an autonomous system. Questioning either the rules or the delineation threatens a return to repression unless the society has the resources and stability necessary to move on to a responsive system. In a responsive system, the political nature of the rules and spheres can become an issue and all trials enforcing those rules and uncritically defending those spheres without consideration of their biased impact on the rights and demands of different groups in the society become bad and political. When moving into a responsive stance, the idea of what can be considered a political trial begins to expand, as does the general feeling that courts are a proper place for the social pressures of change to be addressed. The most significant pressures for a responsive approach in the courts come from within an autonomous approach:

The main competence of autonomous law is its capacity to restrain the authority of rulers and limit the obligations of citizens. An unanticipated result, however, is to encourage a posture of criticism that contributes to the erosion of the rule-of-law. This is not an ideological stance, for the rule-of-law model is more likely to celebrate submission to authority than criticism of it. But the practical operation of the system presses in another direction. As the institutions and procedures of autonomous law develop, criticism of authority becomes the daily occupation of lawmen. This is evident in the technical spirit with which they analyze, interpret, and elaborate the meaning of rules, and in their highly self-conscious commitment to procedural regularity. This commitment puts the courts in the business of defining opportunities for the assertion of claims. This advocacy comes to rival adjudication as the paradigm of legal action. The outcome, however unintended, is a right-centered jurisprudence.[23]

Contrary to this direction is the deeply ingrained commitment an autonomous approach has to formal justice through meticulously followed procedure. But

procedure serves more ends than fairness alone. It is also a resource for limiting access to the courts and for ensuring that the judges' right to the "last word" is invoked with economy and caution. A panoply of rules and doctrines limit standing, defend narrow conceptions of "justiciability," preserve judicial aloofness, stress party initiative and party responsibility, enforce strict criteria of legal relevance, confine the court's authority to the case at hand, and justify deference to political will and administrative judgment.[24]

What happens in a responsive system is that a repressive system is turned on its head. Individual citizens and groups begin to define the public interest and seek substantive justice through the courts. The function of law and the courts becomes that of elaborating and correcting social policies. It involves testing alternative strategies for the implementation of mandates and reconstructing those mandates in light of what is learned. Any trial can be political in the sense that courts can be forums for policy debate, policy formulation, and even policy creation.

RESPONSIVE LAW, POLITICAL TRIALS, AND JUSTICE

Responsive law, then, does not accept the idea of law as a neutral framework, nor does it accept the ideas of law as a sovereign command or the servant of the dominant class. Since these are the most politically and socially popular theories, responsive law occupies a rather unfashionable niche in the theoretical spectrum. We are uncomfortable with it. For many of us, it stretches our common understanding of courts, law, and the separation of powers. This results in its finding expression in some startlingly unregarded cases, which are nevertheless revered in many of the more relaxed circles at the periphery of our society (e.g., universities) as the repositories of some wisdom. For although they play fast and loose with our more traditional and popular concepts of property and liberty, they are superior to the other approaches in two important respects. First, they recognize the social nature of property, and second, they look to the substantive social impact of the law.

The first of these cases we shall consider is *Goldberg v. Kelly*.[25] The Goldberg court decided that terminating "public assistance payments to a particular recipient without affording him the opportunity for a rudimentary hearing prior to termination"[26] was totally unacceptable. "It may be realistic today to regard welfare entitlement as more like property than a gratuity," wrote Justice William Brennan. "Much of the existing wealth of this country takes the form of rights that do not fall within traditional common law concepts of property."[27]

This case was political and responsive because it redistributed wealth and power by redefining property in a responsive way to prevailing social pressures and realities. In fact, property was expressly taken to be a social creation; it was considered an assignment of status among people for social purposes. Moreover, the case sought to do more than procedural justice. It sought to define the public interest in response to social pressures; pressures the Court considered an opportunity for correcting the law so that it might achieve substantive social justice.

Following *Goldberg*, the Court began moving into a more responsive position. First, it held that "a person's liberty is equally protected when the liberty itself is a statutory creation,"[28] because statutory entitlements secure "many of the core values of unqualified liberty,"[29] and because even when laws do not explicitly create property or liberty rights, the courts can recognize a "core" of substantive liberty and property rights implicit in the Constitution. Then, in *Wisconsin v. Constantingan*,[30] the court found a liberty interest "where a person's good name, reputation, honor, or integrity is at stake because of what the government is doing to him."[31] Consequently, due process requirements had to be met before any action was taken by a government to explicitly label a person in a derogatory manner. In *Jenkins v. McKeithen*,[32] the Court said that the public identification of criminals had such a personal, social, and economic consequence that due process obligations were triggered.[33] And in *Wisconsin v. Constantingan* the same thing was said regarding action taken to publicly label someone an alcoholic.[34]

This idea that courts, in response to small pressures and needs, could recognize new properties and liberties not expressly mentioned in any statute or constitution but which reasonably were corollaries of core rights, became so disconcerting that the Supreme Court began to revert to a more autonomous stance. In *Paul v. Davis*,[35] Justice Rehnquist said that an individual's interests where not protected by due process when police distributed his or her name to local merchants as a known and active shoplifter, despite a lack of convictions and an admission that so labeling him "would seriously impair his future employment opportunities."[36] The chief justice distinguished *Wisconsin v. Constantingan* as holding only that a state-conferred right to buy liquor had been interfered with by the posting of one as an alcoholic, not the "core" right to a good name as the Court had originally said. So the court stopped construing and applying policy responsively and returned to a strictly defined sphere of enforcing rights only as explicitly granted by the state.

One disturbing aspect of this case and our autonomous stance in general is the Court's willful ignorance. It purposefully ignored the practical impact of labeling someone a shoplifter and the shift of power that this would entail. State officials could now, with little or no foundation, stigmatize someone for life, which is exactly what the state did in *Bishop v. Wood*[37] and *Codd v. Velger*.[38] In the former, the court said that even if a police officer's "discharge was a mistake and based on incorrect information," there was no involvement of a protected liberty; in the latter, stigmatizing material could be placed in a personal file and circulated to prospective employers without a hearing.

Unresponsiveness has not been limited to ignoring the political and economic impacts of decisions nor the intrinsic purposes of due process hearings; courts have remained stubbornly unresponsive to the idea that economic rights might be connected to constitutional rights. In *Charland v. Norge Division, Borg-Warner Corp.*,[39] the plaintiff was fifty-five years old and had worked thirty years for the defendant corporation, which, with the help of the plaintiff and many others like him, had grown and prospered. The corporation then decided to move away, and as the plaintiff understood it, "at the end I am thrown out of a job unless I move hundreds of miles to another city and start as a new employee behind hundreds of local residents and without either accumulated seniority or pension rights. In the alternative, if I sign a complete release of all rights arising out of my job, I get $1,500. This is fundamentally unfair. And it is a deprivation of my property rights in my job in violation of Article V of the United States Constitution."[40] The Court's response was that "whatever the future may bring, neither by statute nor by Court decision has appellant's claimed property right been recognized to date in this country."[41]

This is a delicate and complex issue and the Court's response is, from a responsive point of view, wrong in all important respects. Most notably, it misses the point of constitutional law in a responsive system and profoundly misapprehends its nature. Constitutions are especially important kinds of law. They enunciate fundamental values, and the role of responsive courts in this area is to at least preserve (if not exceed) those values. This job requires that the courts remain open to the inevitability of change. Especially, it requires them to recognize changes that have already occurred in our patterns of living and formulate the law's meaning so that it ensures the continued survival of our fundamental values in light of that change. So, as Justice Douglas once said:

The place of stare decisis in constitutional law is . . . tenuous. A judge looking at a constitutional decision may have compulsions to revere past history and accept what was once written. But he remembers above all else that it is the Constitution which he swore to support and defend, not the gloss which his predecessors may have put on it. So he comes to formulate his own views, rejecting some earlier ones as false and embracing others. He cannot do otherwise unless he lets men long dead and unaware of the problems of the age in which he lives do his thinking for him.[42]

The point is that fundamental values are important enough to override past policy, and a policy of not recognizing property rights in jobs (even though we could make a strong Lockean argument in its favor), while waiting around for the future to bring such a recognition, ignores the economic realities of our time. Courts are, after all, responsible for the defense of fundamental values against the onslaught of history.

Some people might reasonably argue that a plaintiff's victory in *Charland* would have been a tyrannical interference with personal liberty. Both labor and capital ought to be allowed free interplay and the government should stay out of it. According to this view, the function of government is to provide a framework within which free individuals can come together and interact without worrying about getting stabbed once they turn around.

We are, however, never free. As demonstrated earlier, power (the ability to get things done, to create, to form knowledge, to pursue goals, to overcome obstacles) depends on and does not exist without social interaction. Law among necessarily interdependent beings is there to facilitate that interdependence and make it more productive. Law is invented to respond to needs as they occur and not to separate people or allow those who might aid those in need to simply go their own way. As we have said before, this may not always be possible. Circumstances might be so stringent or the society so crisis ridden that a complete responsiveness is impossible. But we do not find convincing evidence that this is the state of affairs in our own society; cases such as *Charland* occur in a plentiful economy coupled to a mature political system capable of responding effectively, efficiently, and fairly to the obvious social and economic problems *Charland* embodies.

But, as we have argued earlier, we as a society have not quite turned the corner on being responsive. We are still ambivalent about how political such cases as *Goldberg* and *Charland* are, and so we sometimes strike out boldly to address the structure of society that enforces political, social, and economic advantages and disadvantages by recognizing such issues as the proper preserve of courts. At other times, however, we reign ourselves in, convinced that this is really a political matter to be handled by legislatures.

Remember, responsive systems are unremittingly and unabashedly political, and they are pluralist by definition. Courts should be looked on as opportunities for political participation by individuals, small groups, or people so dispersed geographically or socially that they would have difficulty organizing to pursue their interests in more traditional ways. Their purpose is a thorough-going justice, fine-tuned to the most precise needs, rather

than a broad justice aiming in the right direction on the whole but failing
in particular instances out of sheer necessity (e.g., necessities born of social
experiences justifying repressive and autonomous approaches). Courts, in
brief, are to be a particular kind of political forum; a truly democratic forum
dedicated to the idea of individualized justice and as open and freely accessible as ever we can imagine.

WHY WE ARE AMBIVALENT

The responsive system is most seductive, so you might wonder why we
would hesitate or defend the autonomous aspects of the system we labor
under today. The responsive approach allows courts to consider merit, equality, liberty, need, and utility on a case-by-case basis for the widest possible
set of imaginable interests, thus maximizing individual utilities and the public
welfare to the greatest possible extent. It envisions an enormous common
law system of great variety, coping with a complex and unpredictable environment. It envisions the law as a social learning mechanism with decision-
making power dispersed throughout our society, modifying itself under con-
tinual feedback from an involved public. However, it involves a system so
intricate, vast, and complex that it does not fit neatly into the public imagination, and this is its central failure. Coming to terms with a centralized,
hierarchical, authoritative system is much easier, although its limitations are
widely recognized. It will take time for people to organize their thoughts
around this more fluid idea.

Moreover, when the law begins facilitating, it stops ordering people
around. Law no longer is sets of determinate standards, and as that happens,
many fear that others will simply do as they please and that law will lose its
authority and become impotent. Nonet and Selznick worry, for example,
that

there is a specter of a multitude of narrow-ended, self-regulating institutions, working
at cross purposes and bound to special interests; or a system impervious to direction
and leadership, incapable of setting priorities; of a fragmented and impotent polity
in which the very idea of public interest is emptied of meaning.[43]

This is an important concern, but the problem is not inherent in vast, self-
organizing, pluralist systems. It is a result of the same peculiar philosophy
of some of the contradictions we looked at before. People can, of course,
learn the sort of narrow interest grubbing that worries Nonet and Selznick.
But that learning comes from laws, religions, educational institutions, and
a media that teaches competition rather than co-operation, self-aggrandize-
ment rather than civic virtue, deference to the high and powerful, and profit
before performance or quality. All of this is called not only loyalty and
morality, but also good, hard-headed, rational thinking.

What we need is a change of habit and mind, and a change in the reluctance of those finding security, identity, and profit in less open systems. Without these changes, a responsive system would not work because everyone would not understand it or how to make it work. We are at present ambivalent to responsive systems of law because our laws and social institutions are partly responsive and partly autonomous and not enough of either to strike a definitive posture.

CONCLUSION

We have argued the inextricability of politics and law, examined characteristics that help us to decide what serves as a political trial, and provided a means of determining what might justify political trials in different contexts. We will now use this framework to evaluate trials on specific topics that we believe either have strong political dimensions or are mostly political and little of anything else. The specific cases we will examine involve first the establishment and free exercise clauses of the Constitution and then the legal rights, duties, and responsibilities that our courts have defined regarding health care access. We believe that these cases reflect the interplay among government, religion, and science in our society and that this interplay is the primary determinant of our social order. Politics, religion, and science embody our most revered practices and our most valued techniques for determining what the truth is about our world. Consequently, they determine who should have what authority and what ought to constitute the proper distribution of power at any given time. Each employs a language and a type of discourse accepted as authoritative and each offers different and often contending modes of action for getting, retaining, and employing power.

Scientific, religious, and political discourse is diffused throughout the entire society and is consumed at different levels by everyone. Consequently, the institutions that produce them become the focus of social, political, and economic demands for such "truths" as will prove effective in making things happen. Truths effective in one universe of discourse (e.g., science) are often seized upon for use in another (e.g., politics) with predictably curious results (e.g., Social Darwinism), which while in fashion define the priorities of who gets what, when, and how (e.g., successful entrepreneurs get the immediate advantages so that the benefits of their endeavors might eventually trickle down to us all). As the truths each produces become the subject of debate, confrontation, and ideological struggle, the discourse of each often circulates through the courts in an attempt to preclude resistance, close loopholes, or facilitate compromise so that the struggle does not disable the society and prevent it from accurately, efficiently, and fairly attaining desired ends. At this point, the courts play the political role of confirming, defining, redefining, shaping, or opposing the current practices that constitute the extant social order as worked out through the interplay of government, science, and religion. Science, politics, and religion are thus the essence of our civilization, and analyzing their interplay in the courts, will demonstrate the usefulness of our framework and allow us to make some suggestions for change at facilitating justice.

NOTES

1. P. Nonet and P. Selznick, *Law and Society in Transition: Toward Responsive Law* (New York: Harper and Row, 1978).

2. Ibid., 25.

3. Ibid., 55–56.

4. Ibid., 89–92.

5. Ibid., 36.

6. J. Rawls, *A Theory of Justice* (Cambridge: Harvard University Press, 1971), 38.

7. Ibid.

8. Ibid., 372.

9. See J. Duncan and M. Dermott, "The Trial of Sir Thomas More," *The English Historical Review* 312 (July 1964); G. R. Elton, *Policy and Police: The Enforcement of the Reformation in the Age of Thomas Cromwell*, (Cambridge: Cambridge University Press, 1972), 400–420.

10. W. C. Barrett, ed., *The Trial of Jeanne d'Arc: A Complete Translation of the Text of Original Prevements* (London, England: Rutledge and Sons, 1931); G. de Santillana, *The Crime of Galileo* (Chicago, IL: Chicago University Press, 1956).

11. See S. G. Brandon, *The Trial of Jesus of Nazareth* (New York: Stein and Day, 1968).

12. L.R. 14, Q.B.D. 273 (1884).

13. Ibid., 274.

14. M. Walzer, *Religion and Regicide: Speeches at the Trial of Louis IV*. Cambridge Studies in the History of Theory of Politics (Ann Arbor, MI: University of Michigan Press, 1982).

15. For this and other examples see T. B. Howell, *A Complete Collection of State Trials and Proceedings from the Earliest Period to the Year 1783*, vol. 4 (London: R. Bagshaw, 1809–1926), 1000–1011.

16. Ibid.

17. *Armstrong v. U.S.*, 421 U.S. 910 (1971).

18. D. Berrigan, *The Trial of the Catonsville Nine* (Boston: Beacon Press, 1970), 100.

19. Ibid., 103–104.

20. See *More v. McNamara*, 387 F.2d 862 (D.C. cir. 1967), *cert. denied*, 389 U.S. 934 (1967); *McCarther v. Clifford*, 393 U.S. 1002 (1968); *Holms v. U.S.*, 391 U.S. 936 (1968); *Atlee v. Laird*, 347 F. Supp. 689 (E.D.P.A., 1972).

21. This case was reported in R. Neely, *Why Courts Don't Work* (New York: McGraw-Hill, 1983), 21–28.

22. Ibid.

23. Nonet and Selznick, *Law and Society in Transition*, 73.

24. Ibid., 67.

25. 397 U.S. 254 (1970).

26. Ibid., 255.

27. Ibid., 262, note 8.

28. *Wolff v. McDonnell*, 418 U.S. 539 (1974).

29. *Morrissey v. Brewer*, 408 U.S. 471 (1972).

30. 400 U.S. 433 (1971).

31. Ibid., 437.

32. 395 U.S. 411 (1969).

33. Ibid., 424.

34. 400 U.S. 477 (1971).

35. 424 U.S. 693 (1976).

36. Ibid., 697.

37. 426 U.S. 341 (1976).

38. 97 S.Ct. 882 (1977).

39. 407 F.2d 1062 (6th Cir.); *cert. denied*, 395 U.S. 927 (1969).

40. Ibid.

41. Ibid.

42. W. O. Douglas, *The Record of the Association of the Bar of the City of New York*, vol. 4 (1949), 153–154.

43. Nonet and Selznick, *Law and Society in Transition*, p. 37.

Chapter Five

Political Trials, Science, and Religion: The Proper Relationship between Church and State

The institutions of science and religion regularly announce rival visions of the public order and continually struggle with each other to have their respective truths actualized in social practice. Competition between the two is sometimes subtle, sometimes intense, but always present. Fundamental differences in how these two institutions define, organize, and evaluate reality make this tension inevitable. Such differences lead to different ideas of authority, power, and obedience. Consequently, their individual visions of the proper public order are resistant to compromise, and the rivalry between them must be continually worked out in practice.

For several reasons, it is important to work out this rivalry and to stabilize the competition between the two, integrate each institution into our social strategies, and ensure that each is related to government in a positive way. First, we must integrate science, religion, and government because we know from experience that each is especially good at one specific thing, both of which we must have to devise a workable social order, and both of which a good government must have to get things done. On the one hand, we must have an "intellectual regime." Getting things done requires a set of practices accepted as the best at authoritatively producing knowledge and meaningfully forming that knowledge into a coherent, useable whole. Usually, we think of the institutions and discourses of science as the best at providing this regime in our society. At the same time, getting things done requires more than knowledge. It requires a coherent set of values and priorities. For us, the institutions and discourses of religion are a primary source of this "moral regime." We cannot get our bearings in the world and organize ourselves to get things done without first weaving together these two regimes and then securing them in their proper places in the social order through normal governmental processes.

Second, in trying to maintain some order, our government must accommodate two broad categories of fanatics. On the one hand, there are those believing that the quality of our lives depends on the part our society plays in the see-sawing success of a wrathful and loving God at odds with evil in the world. These people energize our religious institutions, and it is primarily through a positive relationship with those institutions that our government draws these people into society and stabilizes their resistance to secularism. On the other hand, there are those believing in the pursuit of pure knowledge, unsullied by moral law, and culminating in a rationally engineered Eden. Providing scientific institutions with a meaningful way of participating in government incorporates these people into our strategies for getting things done.

Finally, our experience tells us that whenever government stumbles in its performance or retreats from its role in organizing and securing the power relationships in society, science and religion quickly move to take over. Every new vision of the public order offered by science or religion is actually a claim that it can provide an effective and superior intellectual, moral, and governmental regime. This leads to much confusion, such as eugenic sterilization based on variations of Social Darwinism and the teaching of "Creation Science," in public schools. Without the forums of good government through which the contending discourses of science and religion can be circulated for authoritative mediation, integration, and assignment to their proper places, we tend to forget that moral reasoning cannot devise an artificial heart and that the scientific method cannot discover the meaning of life. So to get things done, we must have both institutions functioning in some workable mix, and we must have government rationally deciding what that mix should be at any given time.

The courts are one governmental forum playing an important role in establishing the most workable mix. In fact, given the intense dedication each fanaticism engenders, the working out of the power relationships between them must always be a matter for the courts. A proper mix is a delicate and elusive thing, changing with context, experience, and purpose. Take away the step-by-step, careful, piecemeal adjustments that in our system only occur in courts and we have little hope of attaining a mix sensitive to current social, political, and economic needs. What, then, ought to define the proper mix or to guide the courts in making such a determination? In this chapter, we will look at the major views on this issue, critique them, and draw implications for how the courts should act when fulfilling their proper political role in defining and adjusting the power relationships that constitute our social order.

THE RELATIONSHIP OF RELIGION AND SCIENCE TO GOVERNMENT

In *Democracy in America*, Alexis de Tocqueville argues that "religion, which never interferes directly in the government of American society, should nonetheless be considered as the first of their political institutions, for although it did not give them the taste of liberty, it singularly facilitates their use thereof."[1] Religion and its institutions provide a framework within which freedom can be exercised without fear of anarchy. It teaches free, independent individuals mutual respect, self-restraint, and some concept of justice, and it lends a purpose to human action.

De Tocqueville's view echoes historically among political scientists, historians, sociologists, anthropologists, and theologians. Sociologist Robert Bellah wrote, for example,

It is one of the oldest sociological generalizations that any coherent and viable society rests on a common set of moral understanding about good and bad, right and wrong, in the realm of individual and social action. It is almost as widely held that these common moral understandings must also in turn rest upon a common set of religious understanding that provide a picture of the universe in terms of which the moral understandings make sense.[2]

Similarly, jurisprudential scholar Sir Patrick Devlin has argued that "without shared ideas on politics, morals, and ethics no society can exist" and that in the West the Christian religion holds a primary place in the inner life of positive and moral law.[3] These writings and many more[4] argue a single point: Religion in general (and in America the Judeo-Christian tradition in particular) legitimizes institutions in some cosmic sense; gives meaning, aspiration, and limit to individual behavior; and in democratic societies such as America, constitutes a set of hidden presuppositions behind the whole structure of social and political thought. It is this more or less internalized set of norms, values, and affectations that makes democratic life possible by reducing the need for external constraints on behavior.

This view argues that religion ought to have a favored position in the social order or that at least it ought to be afforded some special accommodation. Religion is the first among our institutions because in a democratic society all others are at risk without the foundation and context it provides. It is politically and socially necessary not only to allow religion a great deal of latitude to proselytize, expound, and generally thrive, but to provide a positive, if not nurturing, environment for its activities.

Three things about this view are particularly interesting. First, the view is "universal consequentialist." All free, democratic societies are facilitated by a common moral understanding. Moreover, political goals are thought of in universal, abstract terms. "Freedom," for example is generally thought of as meaning the same thing in all contexts, cultures, and times. It is considered an internally developed virtue that might be facilitated by tangible external constraints, usually on one's self as well as on others. Second, this view assumes that those common moral standards necessarily (in an empirical and normative sense) rest on a transcendental foundation. That is, common ethical or moral standards require some cosmic underpinning to be justifiable as standards. Finally, it assumes that political behavior and political discourse require a single authoritative framework within which to occur. Without this framework, behavior would be "nasty and brutish." Moreover, there would be no common understanding to base discourse on as we strategically interact. It would be difficult to even talk about what goals we might pursue and what values we might promote (let alone *how* we might do so) outside one inclusive authoritative framework.

Against this view, it is most often urged that what informs American political behavior and discourse (given the Enlightenment) is not internalized Judeo-Christian religious norms but "scientific" or "rational" inquiry combined with an incremental pragmatism (means/ends calculations toward modest and immediate goals). Thomas Jefferson was an early proponent of this approach. Rationalism and pragmatism run persistently through his justifications of both republican democracy and tripartite government.[5] Even his justifications of rebellion and civil disobedience are distinctly pragmatic.[6]

A more modern example is John Dewey. Rational and pragmatic incrementalism are one foundation of his political and philosophical "reconstruction" of society.[7] Still more recently, M. M. Marty argues that "while Protestants pointed with pride to their achievements [in American history] they hardly realized that the typically rationalist view of the irrelevancy of theological distinctions in a pluralist society was pulling the rug out from under them." This means, continued Marty, "that the Enlightenment prevailed over the forms American religion took in its development from Calvinism."[8] Similarly, historian-theologian J. Raroutunian argues that Christian orthodoxy in the United States

has been a toure de force, which has persisted and flourished largely either as a denial or as an escape from American experience. . . . Its supernaturalism and appeal to authority; its pitching of Christian doctrine against the ideas of the scientific community and its advocacy of faith as against intelligence; its severing prayer from work and the sacred from the secular have made orthodoxy an alien mind in a land which has equated industry and method with good things and common prosperity.[9]

Finally, D. H. Meyer argues, in *The Democratic Enlightenment*, that while there have been attempts in American history to undo the Enlightenment,

when all is said and done, the fact remains that the Enlightenment could be contained but not extinguished . . . the Enlightenment marked a significant stage in the coming of modernity, the application of the techniques and assumptions of the new science in areas of metaphysics, ethics, and social thought. It was part of the wider culture's assimilation of the scientific revolution . . . the rationalism of the Enlightenment could be ridiculed and condemned but its rationality one just had to learn to live with.[10]

According to this view, the presuppositions informing, legitimating, and giving meaning, aspiration, and limit to social, economic, and political behavior are empirically founded theories open to ongoing adjustments. By increasing the verisimilitude (the empirical fit) of our theories, we can come to understand the empirical forces at work around and within our political system. This, in turn, will allow us to perceive the most efficient and effective ways of pursuing goals and promoting values. It would also inform us about which goals and values are practicable. Through experiment, *a priori* goals and values should bump up against reality and be modified accordingly. What is needed is experiment and a general loosening of restrictions on thought and behavior.

This means, of course, that church and state are not functionally connected institutional authorities. At best, churches are voluntary experimental associations within the nation competing with thousands of others. At worst, churches impede free experiment and a rational approach to problem solving and should perhaps be excluded from the realm of political action altogether.

Three points should be noted about this view. First, the view is "situationalist." Experiment in differing situations is necessary to determine what facilitates freedom and democracy. Moreover, "freedom" and "democracy" tend to be defined empirically as, for example, the lack of external constraints or a set of necessary procedures. Second, the view assumes that common standards of behavior must (empirically and normatively) rest on a "scientific" (empirical) foundation. That is, common standards require some materially tangible underpinning to be justifiable. Finally, it assumes that political behavior and discourse need only a procedural framework within which to occur. Science and rationalism will tell us what can be done and how it can best be done. It tells us not only what to do but what to talk about, what are important problems to discuss, and what are reasonable solutions.

Regardless of where our sympathies lie, problems and a persuasive force are recognizable in each view. Moreover, given the persuasive force of each as woven into our culture and history, there is no American public order that can actually thrive unless it attains some workable mix of the two. Although elements of one model often predominate in practice, and the basic posture of our current order tends to institutionalize the nonrationalistic universalist view in a favored way, these two models should be viewed as points on a continuum along which our particular order shifts or is capable of shifting in practice, if not in institutional structure. Scientifically or religiously "pure" orders are rarely given serious consideration or broad based support, and orders without either are scarcely imagined. These ideas rep-

resent the boundaries against which our society defines itself. The Constitution enshrines freedom of religious association and belief, for example, to
encourage a variety of such associations in counteracting each other's excesses
and to prevent coercion by any single established church. Religious groups
embodying the ideals of a theocracy or based on total commitment or charismatic leadership are there to serve no legitimate social function, and we
tend to exclude them in various ways. The problems inherent with each
view, their persuasive force, and the tendency to exclude pure forms have
implications for courts when adjusting the proper mix in an appropriate way.

The Problems

Being consequentialist, both paradigms undercut the integrity of any moral
stance. The universalist leaves itself and any moral stance derived from it
open to dismissal by empirical evidence that societies can be recognizably
free and democratic despite a plurality of moral understanding. That is, if
it is demonstrable that changing rules or procedures in different empirical
situations increases freedom and/or democracy in that situation, claims of a
universally proper (authoritative) way, become hard to sustain. Consequently, consistent stances about what should be done or the proper church/
state relationship are similarly undercut. By the same token, no moral stance
derived from a situation-specific procedural adjustment can claim any temporal durability.

In being consequentialist, then, each paradigm defeats its own ability to
legitimize discourse to "proper" channels. In defeating one fundamental
purpose of any moral stance or language game, both become insufficient to
our understanding of a "proper" relationship among institutions, values,
rationales, and facts in general and church/state relationships in particular.

In the same manner, both views assume the need for an external justification for their moral propositions. Once again, each paradigm undercuts
itself by claiming either a transcendentally or an empirically good foundation.
Certainly, what is derived as "good" from sequential, empirical, situation-
specific observations can change as those situations change and be contradictory to our ideas of an overall good result. Similarly, any idea of a transcendent good falls to a single instance of evil resulting from the following
of its precepts.

More importantly, the practice of justifying moral propositions in terms
of something outside the users of such propositions is questionable and doing
so can lead quickly to not only puzzlement and confusion but also to an
inability to get things done. For example, it seems clear that articulating
vague feelings of need, injustice, immorality, or at least concern about what
we are doing makes those feelings real to us and at least worthy of consideration, if not fulfillment. People, then, do seem to be the origin of moral
and practical propositions, insofar as they can be articulated and understood.

It is also clear that religious and scientific languages cannot only express those needs, feelings, and concerns but serve them as well by suggesting how we might effectively go about addressing them properly. Consequently, people are limited in fulfilling their needs or acting morally only insofar as they either cannot find within their religious or scientific views and languages meaningful articulations of their needs, or they refuse to look beyond accepted articulations for new explanations and descriptions. Thus, we are only stymied or confused when we take "scientific" or "religious" stances or think in the terms of a "scientific" or "religious" language when we are trying to solve a problem it was intended to address. Similarly, we are puzzled when our problems are not resolved as an accepted "scientific" or "religious" language or stance suggests they should be only if we are unquestionably committed to that particular language or moral stance and so unwilling to adopt another that may prove more effective. In the last analysis, it is human beings who, according to their purposes, not only articulate moral propositions but justify them and declare them good or valuable. Similarly, what is accepted as empirically necessary is largely a judgment by human beings worked out under the exigencies of their needs in varying circumstances. Unfortunately, both views purporting to define what motivates, legitimates, limits, and gives meaning to political behavior and discourse in America evince a lack of confidence in the human being. Both reduce human beings to dependent variables responding to either cosmic or empirical dictates insofar as they act "properly." The idea that human beings might organize, prioritize, and define what is proper in terms of their own aspirations and perceptions of what life should be like is given short shrift. It is assumed that without cosmic or empirical discipline human society would degenerate or at best stagnate, but certainly never progress.

Consequently, neither religion nor science can guide us in working out the proper church/state relationship. The proper relationship and mix of morals, rationality, empiricism, and intuition must be worked out in terms of human purposes rather than appeals to either empirical necessity or transcendental authority. Courts, for example, in deciding whether a particular relationship between church and state is proper must look to how that relationship is operating in society, how it is integrated into the strategies for getting things done, who it serves, and what power relationships it supports.

The Strengths

Paradoxically, the force of the universalist and situationalist views is that they can both work. They can work because the politics/religion/science relationship is "open" in nature and therefore subject to human organization and justification (which both views deny). The relationship does not possess its own natural essence. Rather, its meaning, point, function, and extent changes with the objective and subjective context of human beings. Consequently, both views are meaningful because both present concepts of the science/church/state relationship and the proper mix of values and rationality that we have seen working in practice at different times. Thus, our ideas of the "proper" mix are built out of cases of great variety that have actually worked to get things done in different contexts. These cases have overlapping conditions, but nothing approaching necessary and sufficient attributes for the specification of a single, set relationship, model, or paradigm. Whether there is at any time a proper mix depends on how familiar the instant relationship is in terms of the overlapping similarities it shares with previous experience and how that mix works to effectively circulate power. The question is not only does it work, but do we recognize this as a proper relationship or is it too far from the familiar?

Fundamentally, people disagree about the nature of a proper mix because each has worked in different contexts and because the idea of a proper mix serves different, though not unrelated, functions for different individuals and groups. For some, it legitimizes and gives purpose and meaning. For others, it serves as an illustration of the necessary conflict and competition for citizen loyalty inherent in a pluralistic society. For still others, it is a means of balancing rational approaches to life and society with spiritual approaches.

The idea of the proper mix and the consequent relationship among church, science, and state in America is historically so internally complex and open that different individuals and groups have looked at the same relationship and, according to their purposes, recognized different elements of the relationship as the paramount, the only important, or the most proper elements of the relationship. Moreover, different groups and individuals have valued highly certain arrangements, recognized rival claims, and appreciated the rival view. They recognized that they must work to maintain their view against the opposition of the other and that perhaps no resolution through argument alone is possible. In brief, the proper relationship among church, state, and science has always been "essentially contested" in our society.[11] This contested nature of the proper mix and the fact that the force (meaningfulness) of both sets of arguments about the proper mix derives from the anthropocentric nature of the process engaged to discover a proper mix helps us to understand the motives and justifications for maintaining the contested nature of the church/state relationship in America. In addition, we might understand the problems with institutionalizing one paradigm over the other.

IMPLICATIONS FOR THE CHURCH/STATE RELATIONSHIP

As we have argued, the world for human beings is, as Hegel put it, "a unity of the given and the constructed," and it is difficult to determine at any given point exactly what is given and what is constructed. The more deeply implanted the social laws and humanly constructed proper procedures and relationships, the more like natural laws ("religious" or "scientific") they appear. We are inclined to say that it is "irrational" or "sinful" to contradict these "deep structures." It is fascinating, then, that we often find ourselves accepting contradictory ideas of science, religion, state, and the proper relationships among them.

We hold such contradictory ideas because our concepts of each of these things was formed through exposure to the use of their signifying terms in a variety of contexts. Sometimes the words were used in such a way as to suggest and reinforce the universalist view. At other times, the context and words were derived from and implied the situationalist idea. We learned the "proper" uses of each term, and with this the "proper" mix and the "proper" relations between church and state, knowledge and values, and rationalism and intuition, by experiencing the use of these terms in all the subtle shadings of context we encountered daily. There was no more similarity among those usages than there was among any two situations.

Still, we somehow understand the idea of a proper mix or relationship and make decisions about individual instances. Similarities of various and changing sorts are enough for us to understand when the boundaries of our understanding of the proper mix have been crossed. We are only perplexed when, in some quest for unity or conceptual tidiness, we try to bring all uses of the terms and all instances of the relationships among them under a single structure of language or thought. Invariably, problems are encountered and something is lost (in terms of social advantages and personal understanding) in this procedure; particularly so in the case of our understanding of the proper church/state relationship.

For example, given this human ability to hold contradictory concepts of a proper mix or relationship according to their purposes, there are certain social advantages justifying the failure of a society to choose finally a church/state relationship and authoritatively establish one as proper.[12] The most important, perhaps, is that some optimum, complex interrelationship may only be achievable or sustainable through a continuous competition. Conceivably, any particular form of the relationship has roles to play (1) in pluralist behavior (e.g., group competition for loyalty and influence), (2) in the fundamental or "deep structure" of our society (the fundamental organizing principles of society), (3) in the institutional dispersion of social functions (e.g., the provision of charitable relief), and (4) in the individual behavior of citizens. The nature of the relationship may necessary be different in satisfying each role. As far as individual behavior is concerned, either church or state (or something else) might predominate as motivator, justifier, or exemplar. In the pluralist setting, it may be necessary for each to compete as equals. Structurally, the state may predominate in establishing the proper distribution for fundamental social rights, duties, and powers, while institutionally the church may predominate in providing certain social needs (both psychological and material). Consequently, the concept of a proper mix or relationship must be variable and open. If it is not, this social advantage is lost in a drive for conceptual elegance, neatness, or consistency.

Consider for example, some implications of institutionalizing either the universalist or situationalist view in terms of Nonet and Selznick's characteristic postures of the American legal system. Remember, the universalist approach posits transcendental moral standards or at least some cosmic underpinnings justifying our moral guidelines. It also argues that political, social, and economic behavior require an authoritative framework within which to occur if people are to remain civil and that we cannot even talk about proper goals, values, and procedures without that framework. Finally, these cosmic norms must be internalized to make democracy possible and must constitute the deep structure of a society, the hidden presuppositions behind the whole structure of political, social, and economic thought and behavior.

These ideas are understood by Nonet and Selznick to constitute "an enduring source of repressive law. "¹³ They do not think that shared moral values are necessarily all bad. They can be a resource for the maintenance of a nonrepressive order if properly understood and applied. As long as such norms and values are pursued in a context or dialogue, persuasion, and respect for questioning and dissent, they function positively. The problem is that the moralism of the universalist approach always threatens to build a disposition to punish into any legal system. Moral ideas quickly become identified with a "fixed image of the social order," and when fundamental ideas are identified with the performance of specific duties, any deviation, in acting or aspiration, from those duties and that image becomes an occasion for punishment.¹⁴

This possibility is illustrated by the examples of bad political trials discussed so far. Briefly, we saw it reflected in the black and white thinking, increased deference to officialdom, erotico-thanotopic imagery, and legal moralism traced through the history of our legal system in earlier chapters. The problem with institutionalizing the universalist model is that tolerance is a delicate social phenomenon at best, and universalist institutions are devices prone to facilitate the transition to intolerance.

On the one hand, the situationalist view can support the autonomous law model and the responsive law model, depending on which of its premises we stress. From situationalist premises, a society might separate law from politics and establish a rule-oriented, procedurally elaborate order in which regularity and fairness are stressed over substantive justice, and fidelity to law means strict obedience to the narrowest, most technical reading of statute and precedent. On the other hand, the same premises might lead a society to stress the purpose of rules over their technical meanings and to establish a flexible, experimental legal order focusing on correcting and changing social institutions with a view toward solving immediate problems.

With regard to politics and religion, we might respond to any given situation by taking the view that law and religion should function apart. They should form differentiated institutional spheres to respond in different ways to different situations. The authority of each would be contained within a definite ambit. Each should be free of the other, and so each would enjoy a certain autonomy within its defined sphere. The law's sphere might be limited to a rational, incremental adjustment of competing interests toward modest mutually acceptable goals, and religion's sphere might address only the human spirit and its quest for development.

The problem is that when the human purposes for integrating religious institutions into the political and social relationships that circulate power become secondary to a rule-oriented formalism, rules are not adapted to social facts but construed in the abstract. When institutional integrity is the primary value, laws are not understood as guides or principles to be contextually interpreted and applied so as to produce results in line with our expectations, but as narrow and precise axioms that can be satisfied by a formal observance derived from a strictly logical, deductive reasoning unaffected by outcome. Thus, on the one hand, this autonomous form of the situationalist approach can support and justify court decisions helping to define the power relationships between church and state, such as those keeping prayer out of public schools and taxes on church property out of public coffers. On the other hand, it can also justify a retreat from the role of a co-equal branch of government responsible for defining power relationships and administrative will of the other two branches evident in cases such as those of the "Catonsville Nine" and *Goldberg v. Kelly.*

Alternately, stressing human purpose by regularly adapting the law to the facts of given situations can foster a simple instrumentalist jurisprudence and threaten the institutional integrity of the courts. This occurs in two ways. First, subordinating doctrine to the achievement of social ends and opening the courts to the interplay of social forces reduces the ability of courts to moderate the power of sheer numbers on the one hand and public and private institutions on the other. Second, because administrators anxious to attain desired ends will seek the most efficient routes, and because many in society will begin to feel uncomfortable with the apparent loss of values and consistency accompanying a goal-oriented jurisprudence, an impulse to a more repressive law approach will occur. Administrators will experience the temptation to overlook and become less sensitive to those whose rights and interests are negatively affected by an otherwise efficient plan of action, and many in society (to some extent as a result of this administrative dynamic) will begin to call for the imposition of a set of absolute values as one way of reining in what may seem to be a rogue society.

So, it is apparently undesirable to institutionalize either the universalist or the situationalist approach even though each meets the shortcomings of the other and each serves important social functions. The only thing we can possibly do in such a situation is to ignore the law of the excluded middle and institutionalize both simultaneously. This can be accomplished through a discriminate and selective responsiveness. By a commitment to distinctive purposes and values that together set the standard for a contextual, outcome-oriented criticism of calls for change and our established practices, we can maintain the integrity of our courts and their openness.

Regarding the proper church/state relationship, this must be decided contextually, not abstractually, and we must realize that in making our decisions our values and our purposes are each equally part of all contexts. Unfortunately, our courts have been neither discriminating nor selective in their responsiveness to religious institutions. Instead, they have been especially solicitous. They have worked out a "special relationship" between church and state that abates the integrity and the openness of our courts and that makes it unnecessarily difficult to alter the pattern of integration among church, state, and science to get things done. Specifically, our courts favor religious institutions through (1) the "preferred position" of religious institutions embodied in the idea of a "zone of required and permissive accommodation," (2) the idea that religious groups as part of the community should share in benefits that the government accords the public generally while being exempt from certain burdens the government also distributes to the general public, and (3) the idea that religious groups might espouse and work politically for nearly any political program sincerely based on their religious beliefs, regardless of how inimical it might be to a free, democratic society of competing interests. These special favors violate some of our most basic values, frustrate the pursuit of some of our most noble purposes, and work contrary to some of our most basic interests.

THE ZONE OF PERMISSIBLE AND REQUIRED ACCOMMODATION

Historically, the courts have interpreted the First Amendment's "establishment" and "free exercise" clauses in terms of two fundamental principles: voluntarism and separatism.[15] Preventing compulsion, direct or indirect, in matters of belief is perhaps more fundamental.[16] Nevertheless, separatism has long been considered important according to three rationales. First, the "evangelical" view has historically worried that worldly corruptions might consume churches if separation was not ensured.[17] Second, the "realist" view has been that public and private secular interests must be protected against "ecclesiastical deprivations and incursions."[18] Third, the "free market" view holds that religious and secular interests should compete among themselves to their mutual advantage.[19] These, then are 2 fundamental values tied to articulated interests that should control court responsiveness to religious institutions as they seek to further their interests and values in strategic interaction with other groups and institutions.

A separatist doctrine, however espousing that "government cannot utilize religion as a standard for action or inaction because [the First Amendment] prohibits classification in terms of religion either to confer a benefit or impose a burden" has never been followed.[20] Instead, courts allow religious classifications to relieve religious groups and individuals of the direct and indirect burdens of public policy.[21] Hence, the creation of a "zone of required accommodation."[22] In addition to a required accommodation of religious interests, the present approach also provides for certain "permissible" accommodations. Thus, it is permissible for school authorities to allow release time for children seeking religious instruction as long as the instruction occurs somewhere other than on school property.[23]

These zones of accommodation stand in the face of real social and individual concerns. In *Wisconsin v. Yoder*, old order Amish were extended the right to withdraw their children from public schools after the eighth grade in order to train them informally for a rural life in keeping with the tenets of their religion.[24] Consequently, the state was required to accommodate the religious beliefs of this relatively small sect within its policy options, goals, and values.

This is, of course, one way of understanding the free exercise and establishment clauses. But surely there is a justifiable social interest (as well as the personal individual interest of the children, as Justice Douglas argued in dissent) in offering an opportunity to the children to develop independent life styles and pursue options potentially at odds with the views and aspirations of their families and religious mentors. *Yoder* arguably contends with such democratic ideals as the right to self-determination and personhood recognized in our law and understood in our political theory as a fundamental human right.[25]

Moreover, it has been argued by the courts that groups espousing and working to effect political ideas fundamentally at odds with democratic values and interests are not entitled to First Amendment protection.[26] The rationale has been that "individual liberties fundamental to American institutions are not to be destroyed under pretext of preserving those institutions."[27] It has seemed a contradiction to the courts to protect political movements (e.g., communism) whose purpose is to do away with the guarantees under which they claim protection.

Interestingly, no such argument was made in *Yoder*. It seems that the zones of accommodation may in some instances require the protection of religious movements opposed to the fundamental values of our society.[28] Arguably, there are limiting cases, such as *Reynolds*, the Mormon polygamy case. Still, the nature and assumptions of even mainstream American religions are in certain respects contrary to fundamental American values and interests. Certain central elements of our political culture, for example, include the ideas that people can be rational; that rationality is a better foundation for social and individual behavior than tradition, unexamined assumptions, untested axioms, charismatic leaders, or the uncritical acceptance of authoritative pronouncements; and that one good source of rational thought is the everyday experience of ordinary people. Consequently, we also adhere to the idea that authority and power should be decentralized and limited in scope. Individuals should be free to experiment, develop their own values, express and follow their own ideas of the good and true, and finally work out their relationships (e.g., through a "social contract") as their experience and reason suggest.

A political order designed to conform to the demands of mainstream religious commitments would be something quite different. The Judeo-Christian tradition assumes an "organic" community embodying a shared commitment to the establishment of a life involving mutual dependence and assistance in achieving religious goals. Assumptions and axioms are established by either a single source (i.e., the Bible) or that source plus the tradition of practice that has historically accompanied it. These assumptions, axioms, and traditions are interpreted by either a special priesthood or a small community of true believers (an "elect") who have been proven worthy, "born again," or "received a vocation." They are applied through authoritative pronouncements, and people are not really expected to experiment with alternative understandings or applications. A true commitment to this orientation is certainly antithetical to the sort of democratic approach we take and not radically different from the type of communism espoused by those tried during the 1950s for their Communist affiliations.

The point is not that the Judeo-Christian tradition cannot be integrated into our society's overall strategies for getting things done, nor that the values of our religious traditions are without foundation or import. It is only that, given its antithetical nature, religion ought not to be given pride of place in our courts. Zones of required accommodation amount to a federally imposed affirmative action program singling out for assistance those whose behavior is religiously motivated. Such accommodation does not comport well with the "evangelical," "realist," or "free market" views on the proper church/state relationship and is certainly a far cry from the Supreme Court's refusal to protect the First Amendment freedoms of individuals and groups holding values and interests at odds with democratic values.

THE "PREFERRED" RIGHTS OF
SPEECH AND ASSOCIATION

Among the preferred rights described by the Supreme Court, freedom of association is one derived by implication from the First Amendment guarantees of speech, press, petition, and assembly. This right has not been held to mean that "whatever a person can [lawfully] pursue as an individual, freedom of association must ensure he can pursue with others."[29] Instead, it guarantees a right to join with others in pursuit of goals independently guaranteed by the First Amendment.[30] In brief, the Supreme Court has created a "preferred" protection for religious groups and groups formed for purpose of advocacy, such as political parties, or the expression of points of view.[31]

The special protection afforded by the freedoms of association and speech is more comprehensive for religion than for advocacy or expression. Certain types of expression are proscribed, such as obscenity, and so not covered.[32] Similarly, certain means of communication are proscribed to some but not to religious organizations.[33] Thus, antihandbill ordinances are often invalidated in the case of religious circulars.[34] One justification for distinguishing religious tracts from others is the need for religions to proselytize.[35] Once again, it should be noted that these preferences are given to religion in the face of valued rights to individual privacy and such legitimate local government concerns as controlling fraud, preventing litter, and preventing citizen harassment.

When these concerns have been addressed in the courts, the special position of religious institutions has frustrated an effective protection of individual rights and the pursuit of legitimate governmental purposes. In *United States v. Ballard*,[36] an indictment for mail fraud was brought in California against a small movement whose leader, Guy Ballard, established a large mail order business from which subscribers could receive the secret teachings of the "spiritual masters." Ballard claimed that Jesus shook his hand, sat for a portrait, and chose him to channel the teachings of the masters and reveal the "Mighty I Am Presence." The Court's technical holding was that the sincerity of beliefs could be examined by courts but the truth could not. But the Court was so split in its response and the dissenting opinions were so strong that the effective holding was that neither sincerity nor truth were justiciable. The dissent of Justice Robert Jackson, for example, was adamant about the untouchability of religious institutions. In his view, "we must put up with, and even pay for, a good deal of rubbish" when it comes to religious institutions promulgating their messages. When a second indictment of the movement subsequently appeared before the Court, it was thrown out and the authorities were given "a broad hint that it would be wise . . . to forget the whole thing."[37]

Finally, it is not at all clear that the free flow of commercial information is less valuable to a democratic society than the free flow of religious ideas. As the Court remarked in a different case: "Commercial information is indispensable to the proper allocation of resources in a free enterprise system; it is also indispensable to the formation of intelligent opinions as to how that system ought to be regulated or altered."[38]

RELIEF FROM SOCIALLY DISTRIBUTED BURDENS

Relief from certain social burdens, particularly taxes, has been granted to religious groups under the establishment and free exercise clauses. Two rationales seem preponderant. First, the spreading of religious beliefs could be "crushed and closed out by the sheer weight of the toll of tribute which is exacted."[39] Second, "granting tax exemptions to churches [has] necessarily operated to afford an indirect economic benefit and also gives rise to some, but yet a lesser, involvement than taxing them."[40] In brief, there is concern "with the extent and duration of entanglement of government with religion through taxing. Similarly, a relief from the burden of military service is provided (under appropriate circumstances) to individuals on the basis of religious beliefs."[41] But no such relief is granted those opposed to war on utilitarian, emotional, or humanistic grounds. Overall, the cases in this area established the principle that however compelling a government's secular purpose, if that purpose is even approximately attainable without burden to religious groups then no burden may be enacted.[42] Thus, a unique position is established for religious groups regarding the bearing of socially distributed burdens.

On the other hand, no such unique position is established regarding the sharing of social benefits. "Free exercise" protection is extended against the governmental withholding of economic benefits and the placing of conditions on their receipt.[43] A reasonable alternative to the present relationship might recognize that the religious clauses do not prohibit all taxation but only "destructive taxation." Surely, churches can be taxed without threatening their existence. Similarly, the amount of "entanglement" might be reasonably regulated to preclude overbearing state intrusions. In brief, there is nothing inherent in taxation that implies the demise of either religion or its free exercise.

DANGERS

Our courts, then, seem to have structured the power relationships of our society in such a way as to give religious groups and individuals certain advantages. Because of certain reservations about political involvement, churches have not always nor consistently used these advantages to their maximum extent. Yet potential dangers exist because of this special relationship and something of their force can be historically recognized in the religious fervor of the 1830s, Prohibition, and the current machinations of such groups as the Moral Majority. Listed below are some present dangers:

1. An overbalance of religious examples as to "good behavior" will threaten individual interests in self-determination, personhood, privacy, freedom, and the striving for personal enhancement and self-realization, as they did in *Yoder*.

2. In the process of establishing a unique position for religion, it transferred the church/state relationship from the context in which it is acting to a special context of abstract reasoning. The relationship is considered apart from its actual settings, purposes, impact, and rules or norms that may have been worked toward some optimal mix. In other words, context limits and specifies the view of a proper mix and a proper church/state relationship. Context specifies what can be considered proper in a given case, and the flexibility necessary to get things done is decreased once context is removed. Since we can make sense of what the proper church/state relationship should be only in some context, removing the relationship from context generates paradox and confusion. Cases abound in which courts, speculating abstractly about the proper church/state relationship, regularly lose sight of a meaningful mix of church and state and even lose track of what we mean by "church," "state," "religion," "politics."[44] They, in turn, lose track of the impact of such abstractions on human beings. For example, it is paradoxical and sad that an individual might be exempted from a military draft because of sincere religious convictions but is denied the same consideration if sincere objections were based on reason alone.

3. The present position of religion in our legal structure arguably results in "now too little" and "now too much" of religious and scientific reasoning motivating and limiting factors of behavior. Taking advantage of their structural position, religious groups periodically seek to transcendentalize the political culture, putting the force of law behind their individual moral preferences (e.g., laws against homosexuality, drinking, masturbation, interracial marriage, swearing in public, and the right to read various materials). Alternately, when reactions to these attempts set in, our society tends to become oversecularized, explaining and justifying its actions on mostly instrumental grounds (e.g., the need to preserve the free movement of interstate commerce as justification for many civil rights rulings).

4. The highly abstract rationalizations prevalent in the current approach often produce observable social and political disharmonies and confusions. The concepts and categories of scientific reasoning and religious doctrine abstract different things from the same contexts and make them important for a variety of purposes and goals held by different groups and individuals. As a result, each group regards certain kinds of questions as the proper subject of political and social action. Generally speaking, for example, scientifically oriented groups focus on questions about the way groups are structured within the overall system, the distribution of power and property, legitimacy and how it is attained, the immediate justification of social and political obligations, and the presence or absence of external constraints on behavior. Alternately, religiously oriented groups focus on questions about the quality of life in terms of transcendent values, the transcendent purpose and meaning of life and political behavior, the moral character of citizens and rulers, and the fulfillment of "truth" and "right." As a result of this

narrowing and focusing, our grasp of the political situation and the available solutions may easily be distorted, or we may unnecessarily be put at odds as to the proper issues and answers. This, in turn, can only frustrate the efficient circulation of power necessary to get things done.

5. While the special relationship between church and state may in some contexts promote certain social interests, such as hard work, self-denial, and the exploitation of nature, the same relationship fostering the same ideas in other contexts may function as a limiting factor. A developed capitalism, for example, requires not self-denial but consumerism in order to flourish and measurements of consumer confidence are integral to investment decisions.[45]

6. A special relationship, such as the one the courts have developed, encourages social groups with interests in certain forms of political, economic, or social organization to employ religion and its institutions to lend an aura of sacredness to the advantages they enjoy. As Max Weber suggested, individuals and groups might "assign to religion the primary function of legitimizing their own life pattern and situation in the world,"[46] This, of course, retards the ability of a society to seek new forms for the efficient circulation of power in changing contexts.

7. Periodically recurring religious fervors tend to disrupt legal authority and threaten the integrity of legal institutions. They tend to foster resistance to current practices or the reform of established political and social orders. Of course, whether this increases or decreases the ability to get things done depends on the context in which it occurs. Special relationships between governmental and religious institutions, however, reduce the ability of government and private groups to curb religious fervor in the social interest.

As we have argued, the court, in examining mixtures of church/state relationships, should consider context very closely. In fact, certain distinctions have been made between the meaning of the establishment and free exercise clauses on the basis of what was being done in specific contexts.[47] If a special relationship, however, must be worked out as an assumed mandate of the First Amendment, the abstract question as to the nature of that unique position is always at issue. It transcends the specific relationship worked out in practice. Paradox might, therefore, be expected, and it is not too difficult to find.

Consider, for example, whether the military should spend federal funds in providing chaplains of various denominations. Providing them seemingly violates the establishment clause, while not providing them seemingly violates the free exercise clause. Paradoxically, no matter what is done First Amendment guarantees are violated.

This is a problem only in the abstract, and then only if religion is assumed to hold a unique position as opposed to other institutionally guaranteed rights. Reserve military personnel on normal weekend or annual active duty can hardly be said to be deprived of First Amendment freedoms in these contexts. On the other hand, a "drafted-against-his-will" soldier on the front lines of a raging war without immediate prospects of getting off the line, arguably has been deprived of certain forms of free exercise by the government.

Still, even in severe contexts, chaplains arguably should not be provided. Other constitutional rights are severely restricted by the military, especially in combat situations, and it is clear from the *Goldman* case that certain religious practices must be foregone while in the military, even in times of peace. The argument justifying this is from necessity, and unless religion is thought to hold a unique position among rights, there is no reason that it, too, should not be restricted out of necessity. On the other hand, even if chaplains are considered essential on the front lines, there is no need to expend federal funds to send and keep them there. If certain religious denominations consider a minister's presence essential to free exercise, it seems their responsibility to provide and maintain the minister from their own funds. In short, the paradox is resolvable by placing the question of church/state relationships in context and removing its favored position status.

PRECLUDING THE DANGERS THROUGH GOOD POLITICAL TRIALS

The special relationship between church and state in our system hampers our best attempts at responsible, selective, and discriminate institutional adaptation. Rather than fixing a special relationship, the free exercise and establishment clauses ought to be understood as responses to particular problems and circumstances that express a core value in a context-appropriate way. The re-expression of those core values and purposes under current social, political, and economic pressures ought to be the court's objective. In order not to be arbitrary, such re-expression should (1) be derived from an informed view of our history, culture, values, and traditions, (2) update that view according to what the terms expressing those values and purposes have come to mean given their current usage, (3) cohere with precedent by making sense of our current knowledge and experience in light of what we have done before, and (4) provide a persuasive vision of a coherent world by integrating history, culture, values, tradition, precedent, and the current meanings of the words expressing our core values and purposes with the most likely immediate results and the most likely pattern of systemic effects given the available alternative decisions open to the court.

Once our core values and purposes have been re-expressed in this way, they may be used to critique not only current and traditional practice but proposed changes as well. This allows us a flexibility that is lacking in paying obeisance to abstract special relationships while rationally controlling the possible alternatives courts might adopt. In this way, courts can help define the public interest and provide substantive justice in cases involving religious and scientific practice.

Good, responsive political trials can not only resolve the tension between openness and loss of integrity that plagues the courts, but can also preclude the dangers we presently face because of the special relationship now recognized between church and state.

NOTES

1. A. de Tocqueville, *Democracy in America*, vol 1 (New York: Vintage Books, 1954), 44.

2. R. Bellah, *The Broken Covenant: American Civil Religion in Time of Trial* (New York: Seabury Press, 1975), xi.

3. P. Devlin, "The Enforcement of Morals," *The Maccabaen Lectures in Jurisprudence of the British Academy* (Oxford: Oxford University Press, 1959), 11–12, 23–25.

4. See R. H. Gabriel, *The Course of American Democratic Thought* (New York: Ronald Press, 1956), 26; P. Selznick, "Natural Law and Sociology" in J. Cogley et al., eds., *Natural Law and Modern Society* (Cleveland, Oh. World Publishing, 1966), 158; R. Benedict, *Patterns of Culture* (Boston: Houghton-Mifflin, 1959) 16.

5. J. Somerville and R. Santonin, *Social and Political Philosophy*, "Thomas Jefferson: Letters" (Garden City, N.Y.: Anchor Books, 1963), 250–281.

6. Ibid., 259–260, 277–281.

7. See J. Dewey, *Reconstruction in Philosophy* (Beacon Press, 1948), ch. 8.

8. M. M. Marty, *The New Shape of American Religion* (New York: Harper and Row, 1959), 71–72.

9. J. Raroutunian, "Theology and American Experience,"*Criterion* 799 (Winter 1964).

10. D. H. Meyer, *The Democratic Enlightenment* (New York: Putnam, 1975), 181.

11. For an exegesis of "essentially contested" see W. B. Gallie, *Philosophy and the Historical Understanding* (London: Chatto and Windus, 1963), ch. 8.

12. What follows is a specific application of a more general analysis in W. B. Gallie, *Philosophy and the Historical Understanding*, 166–618.

13. P. Nonet and P. Selznick, *Law and Society in Transition: Toward Responsive Law* (New York: Harper and Row, 1978), 46.

14. Ibid., 48–49.

15. See C. Miller, *The Supreme Court and the Uses of History* (Cambridge: Belknap Press of Harvard University Press, 1969). Also for specific examples see *Committee for Public Education v. Nyquist*, 413 U.S. 756 (1973); *Flast v. Cohen* 392 U.S. 83 (1968); and *McGowan v. Maryland*, 366 U.S. 420 (1961).

16. See *Walz v. Tax Commission*, 397 U.S. 664 (1970); P. Freund, "Public Aid to Parochial Schools," 82 *Harv. L. R.* 1680 (1969).

17. M. Howe, *The Garden and the Wilderness* (Cambridge: Harvard University Press, 1965), 6; P. Miller, *Roger Williams: His Contribution to the American Tradition* (New York, Antheneum Publishers, 1962), 89–98.

18. Howe, *Garden and Wilderness*, 2.

19. R. Hunt, "James Madison and Religious Liberty" 1 *American History Association Report* 165 (1961).

20. R. Kurland, *Religion and the Law* (Cambridge: Harvard University Press, 1962), 18.

21. See *Sherbert v. Verner* 374 U.S. 398 (1913): State must modify its unemployment compensation requirement of willingness to work Mondays through Saturdays in order to accommodate those religiously opposed to working Saturdays).

22. See L. Tribe, *The Constitutional Protection of Individual Rights* (Mineola, NY: Foundation Press, 1971), 821.

23. See *Zorach v. Clauson* 343 U.S. 306 (1952).

24. 406 U.S. 205 (1972). See also H. Raggi, "An Independent Right to Freedom of Association," 12 *Harvard Civ. Rights Civ. Lib. Law Review* 1, 15 (1977).

25. A right to personhood as defined was recognized in *Whalen v. Roe*, 97 S. Ct. 869 (1977). The right was derived from the right to privacy.

26. See *Communist Party v. Subversive Activities Control Board* 367 U.S. 1 (1961).

27. Ibid.

28. There is one early case to the contrary, *Reynolds v. The United States*, 98 U.S. 145 (1878). There it was held that the "establishment" and "free exercise" clauses deprived Congress "... of all legislative power over mere opinion, but was left free to reach actions in violation of social duties or subversive of good order." Cases regarding religious practice, however, are to the contrary, as the *Yoder* and *Sherbert*, cases demonstrate. The only exceptions involve the use of narcotics in the practice of non-Native American religions.

29. H. Raggi, *"An Independent Right to Freedom of Association,"* 15.

30. *Cousins v. Wigoda*, 419 U.S. 477 (1975); *NAACP v. Button*, 371 U.S. 415 (1963).

31. See *Serbain Eastern Orthodox Diocese v. Milivojevich*, 426 U.S. 696 (1976).

32. *Roth v. United States*, 354 U.S. 476 (1957).

33. See *Schneider v. State*, 308 U.S. 147 (1939) and *Martin v. Struthers*, 319 U.S. 141 (1943).

34. *Bread v. Alexandria*, 341 U.S. 622 (1951).

35. See *Murdock v. Pennsylvania*, 319 U.S. 105 (1943) and *Martin v. Struthers*, 319 U.S. 141 (1943).

36. *United States v. Ballard*, 332 U.S. 78 (1944).

37. L. Pfeffer, "Legitimation of Marginal Religions in the United States," in I. Zaretsky and M. Leone, eds., *Religious Movements in Contemporary America* (Princeton, N.J.: Princeton University Press, 1974), 23.

38. *Virginia v. State Board of Pharmacy v. Virginia Consumer Council*, 425 U.S. 765 (1976).

39. See *Murdock v. Pennsylvania*, 319 U.S. 112 Supra note 22 (1943).

40. *Walz v. Tax Commission*, 397 U.S. 664 (1970).

41. *Gillettee v. U.S.*, 401 U.S. 437 (1971).

42. See Tribe, *Individual Rights*, 849 for the analysis of cases in this area arriving at the state principle.

43. See *Sherbert v. Verner*, 374 U.S. 398 (1963).

44. See C. M. Whelan, "Governmental Attempts to Define Church and Religion," *Annals, American Association of Political and Social Science* 32–51 (November 1979), and Tribe, *Individual Rights*, 826–830.

45. J. L. Peacock, *Consciousness and Change: Symbolic Anthropology in Evolutionary Perspective* (Oxford: Basil Blackwell, 1975), 78–82.

46. M. Weber, *Economy and Society* (New York: Bedminster Press, 1968), 491.

47. See generally W. Katz, *Religion and American Constitution* (Northwestern University Press, 1964); D. H. Giannella, "Religious Liberty, Non-Establishment, and Doctrinal Development: Part II, The Non-Establishment Principle," 81 *Harv. L. R.* 513 (1868); R. Cushman, "Public Support of Religious Education in American Constitutional Law," 45 *Harv. L. R.* 333.

Chapter Six

Political Trials, Science, and Religion: Politics and Medical Science

Nowhere is the confrontation between politics, religion, and science more intense than in the fields of medicine and health care. Such scientific advances in the technology of the biological sciences as test tube babies, genetic recombination, the "morning after" pill (RU–846), and the Human Genome Project have promoted visions of power over death, disease, suffering, and the future of human society. Our developing ability to manipulate genes has resurrected the idea that messy moral, political, and economic issues might be resolved by substituting the right nucleotide in the cells of miscreants, dissidents, and the poor. For example, when asked why federal funds given to the Human Genome Project should not be given instead to the homeless, Daniel Koshland, the editor of *Science* magazine, replied, "What these people don't realize is that the homeless are impaired. . . . Indeed, no group will benefit more from the application of human genetics."[1]

At the same time, the effectiveness of modern birth control technologies and the safety of modern abortion procedures has pushed family issues in general and abortion law in particular into the political limelight as part of the "New Religious Right's" program for social reform. The "cult of the playboy" and the freedom of women to experiment sexually outside marriage are seen by coalitions of conservative Protestants and Catholics as the undesirable effects of modern birth control methods and the dissemination of birth control information. Not only are these methods and this information understood to encourage evil behavior, but such information and its concomitant behavior are seen as threatening the family's position as the "fundamental building block of society." This threat is intensified by the ready

access to abortion. The religious right understands conception as the beginning of human life and conducts educational campaigns, exerts pressure on
legislators, and, in extreme cases, launches violent attacks on medical clinics
that perform abortions.

Finally, biological and medical information is becoming a focus of struggle
between individuals and the institutions. The power relationships between
individuals and the courts, for example, is strongly conditioned by the availability of DNA profiles as a forensic tool. Health care providers also desire
access to these profiles to reduce their costs by targeting their services to
those with the best health prognoses. This information is valuable to employers as well. It is a means of reducing insurance costs and hiring applicants
least sensitive to any health hazards that may accompany the job. The possession of knowledge concerning the state of an individuals' DNA, then, is
a major issue affecting hiring, promotion, constitutional guarantees of a fair
trial, and the availability of health care.

Courts are becoming the preferred forum for debating these policy issues
and the preferred political mechanisms for restructuring the power relationships at issue." In the process, they are being asked to distribute scarce
social resources and to define rights affecting our most profound personal
interests. Intense differences are arising about who has what rights and what
responsibilities with regards to privacy, personhood, personal dignity in
death, abortion, health care, and the quality of our lives when we are ill,
aged, or disabled. Conflicts over these issues are exacerbated by conflicts
over who has what access to sophisticated treatment techniques and technologies, how much research money should be directed at which diseases,
and who should be provided with what kinds of health care benefits.

These conflicts are presented by intensely dedicated, often relatively
small, narrowly focused, and often uncompromising interest groups. On the
question of abortion, for example, Americans are deeply divided on the
definition of the issue and the nature of the problem. Does abortion involve
the killing of a human being or the termination of a pregnancy? Does a fetus
have rights? If so, whose rights have priority, the woman's or the fetus'?
When scientific experts were unable to provide conclusive evidence on which
to form a policy concerning these issues, the majority in *Roe v. Wade* worked
out a delicate compromise, attempting to balance carefully the rights of
women and the interest of the state in protecting human life. The result was
a highly charged clash of single-issue politics by conservative religious organizations and feminist groups that is still in progress.

In this context, courts are unable to call effectively on either the "popular
will" or a broadly recognized "higher law." They are caught between the
alternatives of risking a loss of respect from many by being truly responsive
to the underlying life and death problems or trying to maintain their authority
by striking an autonomous stance and removing themselves from the fray.
The result is a series of bad political trials reflecting the vagaries of the

scramble for power among individuals, groups, and institutions whose interests, problems, and concerns focus around medicine and health care. A study of almost any subset of cases in the general health care access field illustrates how the religio-political/economic context can so overlay the real life context as to produce bad political trials (e.g., trials not consonant with the more basic human realities at stake).

In this chapter we will consider first the grass roots, "real life" context within which these decisions are being made. Next, we will examine how the overlay of religious, political, and economic forces arrayed against the grass roots affects court decisions. We will then provide a specific illustration of the tension between the grass roots and the overlay and analyze the way in which the tension skews court behavior and produces bad political trials. Finally, we will suggest ways of using the courts to turn things around with good political trials.

THE CONTEXT

Today there exists a clear imbalance in health care access. In an economic context of plenty, a social context defined by "haves" and "have nots," and a political context in which the vast majority believes that quality health care is a basic human right,[3] courts remain deeply divided on issues of health care access. Our highest court, for example, is torn between the popular will and the dictates of competing political, religious, and economic "higher laws" intensely promoted by politically active, well-funded, and well-connected interest groups.[4] Consequently, along with the other branches of government, the court seeks to evade responsibility for making the tough choices by taking an autonomous stance and passing the responsibility to state legislatures.

The roots of the problem extend to the economic, political, and social optimism, diversity, and richness, of the 1960s. Populist political movements of the time advanced strong arguments for a broad-based, publicly financed health-care program. The core proposition was that every citizen was endowed with a moral right to health care, deserving judicial support and constitutional protection. In this way, ideals of popular will and higher law conjoined to bring about Medicare and Medicaid as a means of enfranchising the poor, the elderly, and the disabled. Legislation, however, to create an all-embracing national health care system failed, primarily because the public will faltered to some extent in the face of rapid inflation and intense opposition from the medical establishment and conservative economic theorists. These interests took effective political advantage of widespread fears of a collapsing economy.[5] In this context, the courts predictably retreated from the responsive law notion that there might be a constitutional right to health care.[6]

The 1970s witnessed a continuing struggle to contain Medicare and Medicaid cost increases resulting largely from escalating hospital costs. The Republican hopes for encouraging the proliferation of HMOs and Democratic hopes for establishing a national health care insurance program were defeated by opposition from most of the health care industry, although the American Medical Association (AMA) played a principle role in defeating Republican hopes, and the Republicans were the sternest opposition to the Democratic plan.[7] Carter administration plans for a 9 percent cap on annual hospital cost increases were similarly frustrated, and attempts at "regional planning for cost efficient utilization" proved politically naive, as regional planning board decisions were either dominated by local provider interests or were overridden by state legislative or executive action at the behest of industry appeals to the state.[8]

In the conservative atmosphere of the early 1980s, popular will waned for most social programs, and no serious efforts to establish a national health care plan were advanced. However, runaway costs (hospital inflation alone ran at over 13 percent)[9], rising taxes, the increasing strains of funding Medicare, and the increasing demands from consumers and third party payers eventually forced Democrats and Republicans into a comprehensive change in Medicare financing for health care delivery.[10] Acting quickly before the health care industry could marshal opposition to a price list, the Medicare Prospective Payment System, based on a price list for "Diagnostic Related Groups" (DRGs), was, with bipartisan and presidential support, appended to certain Social Security amendments and joined with the Tax Equity and Fiscal Responsibility Act of 1982. The goal of this system was to shift the risk of cost containment from the taxpayer to the providers of health care services, primarily hospitals.[11]

Under this present system, hospitals and other qualifying providers of health care are compelled to look for ways to provide care for diagnostically related groups of illness at costs at or below a governmentally established rate. Decisions to admit, transfer, and discharge patients have been affected. The immediate effect was to disenfranchise millions of poor patients from access to quality health care and to allow discrimination against the elderly and disabled on the basis of age and/or disability.[12] In addition, there was a direct effect on the intensity of care provided to Medicare patients. Today's elderly, for example, are faced with increasing costs for copayments and deductibles and increasing limitations on access to care and use of benefits. This, of course, restrains their utilization of health care options for reasons exogenous to the nature of their illness. Similarly, the amount of long-term care (beyond 150 days) available to the elderly is dependent on the ability to purchase private insurance. Only after the exhaustion of private funds are the elderly currently eligible for Medicaid. Health care is now presented as a commodity. A right to buy has supplanted a right to care. The result is that today over 40,000,000 Americans are without insurance or medical benefits. Less than 50 percent of the poor Americans are covered by Medicaid, and 20 percent of the population in America needs health care but have difficulty obtaining it.[13] Since 1986, an average of over one million Americans per year were unable to obtain necessary care because of their inability to pay.[14] In addition, hospitals responded by moving out of primary health care and marketing new services aimed at young to middle-aged people with money (e.g., sleep centers, sports medicine complexes, psychological counseling centers, sexual dysfunction clinics, and obesity clinics).

This state of affairs is largely the result of the government's reluctance to critically review a health care delivery policy that understands health care as a commodity rather than as a right. We must secure this right if people are to have an equal opportunity to advance themselves and secure basic commodities based on merit, ability, and skill. The idea that access to health care should be based on free choice in an open market, allowing supply to respond to demand according to the resources of private decisions, the idea that fees for services should be based on the demand/supply ratio, and the idea that the needy are entitled to an open-ended financing based on the ideology of equal access according to need as defined by patient and physician simply allow legislatures to avoid addressing the difficult question of whether and to what extent access should be regulated. Similarly, executives currently hide behind legislative reluctance to provide funds, partisanship, "administrative problems," and a lack of clarity in health care policy, to smother issues surrounding the ineffective, inefficient, and inequitable distribution of health care in legislative or bureaucratic rules, regulations, and guidelines, while satisfying disaffected groups with rhetorical support. Finally, the courts rely heavily on custom, tradition, and "fate" to avoid addressing the difficult issue of whether a right to health care is fundamental to our idea of ordered liberty. Our government avoids these issues in order to avoid conflict, until it is absolutely certain that it must be confronted. Unfortunately, despite what the cases in this area are currently revealing about what is happening to human beings, the political obstacles to a definitive court response are significant. Then obstacles contribute to a politically understandable judicial reluctance, which leads to bad political trials.

THE CASES

Especially illustrative of how the politico-religious/economic overlay produces bad political trials is that subset of cases dealing with health care delivery for abortions. Not since the 1954 decision in *Brown v. Board of Education*[15], has an issue so dominated the political scene and stirred such division. In this arena, as in the general health care delivery field, courts are unable to appeal to either the popular will or a higher law in articulating a definitive approach. Consequently, they have sought to strike a neutral, autonomous stance, hoping that either something will break or that people will calm down enough for law to be made quietly on a case-by-case basis. Unfortunately, this approach has resulted in some bad political trials.

Consider *Maher v. Roe*[16] and *Harris v. McRae*[17], two core cases invariably cited by lower courts as fundamental law in the health care delivery field. Splitting five to four, along conservative and liberal lines, the Supreme Court held that neither the state nor the federal government was obliged to provide any substantive services for their citizens, including medical treatment and abortions.[18] In brief, the court decided that neither the due process nor equal protection clauses granted it any role in securing individuals rights to health care access. Not only was the existence of such a right completely a matter of legislative discretion, but should a legislature decide to dole out some health care access, it was perfectly legitimate to do so on the basis of a recipient's value. Of course, courts have always recognized a state's power to direct its largess to legitimate governmental interests and ends. But *Maher* and *McRae* together explicitly empower states to make value judgments without limitation and to allocate public funds discriminately to those who happen to agree.

Maher v. Roe was essentially an equal protection challenge to a Connecticut regulation funding the expenses incidental to childbirth, while prohibiting the funding of nontherapeutic abortions. There were two appellants. Susan Roe was an indigent, unwed mother of three whose physician refused to certify that an abortion was medically necessary. Mary Poe was a sixteen-year-old high school junior whose hospital was denied reimbursement for the same reason. In upholding the regulation, the Court reinforced a long-standing countenance of effective disenfranchisement via economics with the old saw that while the Constitution does guarantee certain rights, it does not guarantee either a right to the things those rights imply nor a right to the wherewithal to effectively exercise those rights.

It is true that we live in a society where, for example, freedom of the press does not include a right to literacy. But the Court had been modifying this general rule for some time, recognizing that the impact of such disenfranchisement on liberty and human dignity was simply too great in certain contexts. Such cases included invalidating state court fees and cost requirements that restricted the ability of indigents to bring actions for divorce (*Boddie v. Connecticut*)[19]; requiring that states provide copies of criminal trial transcripts to the indigent and their counsel (*Griffin v. Illinois*)[20]; recognizing a substantive right to participation in the electoral process on an equal footing with all qualified voters (*Reynolds v. Sims*)[21], and invalidating certain state residency duration requirements for the receipt of public benefits (*Shapiro v. Thompson*).[22]

Moreover, *Maher* did not occur in a context in which those who could afford treatment got it while the poor did not. Nobody in the *Maher* context could afford health care. They were all indigent. The question was whether the government could step in and give some people the ability to exercise the choice they had the right to make while denying that wherewithal to others.

It does seem that health care differs from most commodities. Even if we are comfortable with the idea that the Constitution guarantees only an equal opportunity to obtain commodities based on merit, ability, and talent, it is nevertheless clear that while you are in a coma it is impossible to either demonstrate merit or exercise abilities and talents. It seems that some minimal health care access must be provided if equality of opportunity is to be advanced. This is what is meant by a fundamental right, and health care access seems to be a prime candidate for election as a right fundamental to our concept of ordered liberty.[23]

The Court, however, had to ignore the real life context, pierce the darkness of possible penumbra, and distinguish the precedents in order to create autonomous realms for itself and the legislature. *Griffin* and *Boddie* were distinguished because the government monopolized the criminal justice system in the first case and the means of dissolving marriages in the second. The Court reasoned that because of this monopolization, the equal protection clause was violated by the denial of criminal trial transcripts to the indigent and divorces to people simply because they could not pay. There are three troublesome aspects about this distinction. First, while abortions are not performed in government buildings or by government personnel, the government does effectively control the procedure and dictate the requirements for obtaining legal abortions. *Roe v. Wade*[24] saw to that. Second, fees for transcripts and court costs for divorces are not absolute bars to proceeding through the courts. Charitable sources of funds are available on an equally theoretical basis for these purposes and for abortions. Third, just as there is nothing requiring state involvement in prenatal access to medical treatment, there is nothing requiring state involvement in marriage. Therefore, if the court is going to argue that the state's voluntary involvement precludes it from discouraging the poor among the married from getting a divorce, it follows that he state's voluntary involvement in prenatal access to medical treatment precludes it from discouraging the poor among the pregnant from getting an abortion.

This monopolization rationale was a distinct undercurrent in the distinguishing of *Shapiro*, but it was not the core argument. Instead, the Court suggested that *Maher* might have been a close analogy to *Shapiro* had the state denied general welfare benefits to all women who obtained abortions as it had denied them for one year to the indigent who moved across state lines. Funding abortions, the Court said, would be like paying the bus fare for indigents coming into the state.

This is a clever and false analogy. The issue in *Shapiro* was "who gets general welfare benefits," and in *Maher*, it was "who gets medical benefits." In neither case was there a constitutional right to either kind of benefit, but in each case, a recognized constitutional right was directly affected by the denial of benefits to some. The real distinction was that in *Maher* no indigent could get any benefits for abortions, while in *Shapiro*, no indigent could get any welfare benefits for one year. Since the state decided to provide general welfare benefits, *Shapiro* held that such benefits must be provided to the indigent, including those who elected to exercise their constitutional right to move into the state just because welfare benefits were higher across the line. So by analogy, it could be argued that once the state decided to provide medical benefits, it had to provide them to the indigent including those who exercised their constitutional right to an abortion because the benefits make it affordable.

By making these distinctions, the Court reduced its responsibility from that of articulating fundamental, substantive constitutional rights in a major political battle to that of providing a ministerial review of governmental acts. This could be almost mindlessly accomplished by running through a checklist to make sure that "the less demanding test of rationality"—requiring that the distinction drawn be "rationally related to a constitutionally permissible purpose"—was met.[25] In this way, the Court decided that "the subsidizing of costs incident to childbirth was a rationale means of encouraging childbirth."[26] Regarding *Shapiro*, the Court essentially decided that it was proper to pay the bus fares of poor people coming into a state if they have the politically correct priorities. Of course, encouraging childbirth was not the issue. The issue was whether encouraging childbirth among poor women who did not want to be pregnant is a legitimate governmental goal. If so, the next issue was whether refusing medical benefits to those poor people who chose abortion, despite the government's preference, is a rationally related means.

In sum, if *Maher* is not a bad political trial as we proposed above, it is at least a shabby one for several reasons. First, while there is no heavy-handed exaggeration of the danger of "us versus them" thinking, guilt by association, or erotico-thanatopic imagery, there is definitely a good sprinkling of deference to authority and legal moralism. The Court defers and abdicates its responsibilities in saying that "[Roe] implies no limitation on the authority of the state to make a value judgment . . . and to implement that judgment by the allocation of public funds."[27] Certainly this is not so. There are some value judgments that have long been considered outside the state's review. States may not, for example, value men more highly than women or whites more highly than blacks. It may not value religion over atheism and certainly not allocate funds to promote religion. It is not a matter of making value judgments, but whether the government made it constitutional.

Second, it is also clear that emotionalism was meant to overcome reason in *Maher*. The Court reminds us that

a woman has at least an equal right to choose to carry her fetus to term as to choose to abort it. Indeed, the right of procreation without state interference has long been recognized as "one of the basic civil rights of man . . . fundamental to the very existence and survival of the race."[28]

This is, of course, true, but it is not the issue nor relevant to the argument regarding whether poor women should be extended the wherewithal to choose to bear children. It is simply intended to gain emotional support for the Court's argument that the state's regulation constitutes a legitimate attempt to promote childbirth.

Third, *Maher* displays lack of concern for the disenfranchised and an explicitly intentional insensitivity to the underlying social facts creating the core problem. The Court simply dismisses the social realities and the state of the poor when it says: "We certainly are not unsympathetic to the plight of an indigent woman . . . but 'the Constitution does not provide judicial remedies for every social and economic ill'."[29]

Fourth, as we argued above, the social, political, and economic context of the decision calls for a responsive approach. As the Court clearly recognizes, there is no social or political consensus on the issue that might justify adopting a single rule and impressing it on everyone. There is also no suggestion of an economic crisis of such proportion as to require discriminant treatment among the poor, although the Court tries to justify its stance by pretending that there is when it says that "our cases have uniformly accorded the states a wider latitude in choosing among competing demands or limited public funds."[30]

Fifth, the Court ignores its responsibility to act as a co-equal branch and be the "ultimate guardian of the liberty and welfare of the people in quite as great a degree" as the legislature in situations in which the legislatures cannot effectively balance interests because sharp social divisions make it politically impossible to do so.[31] Sixth, the Court knew that *Maher* was not about a state's decision to promote childbirth. The explicit historical, social, and political reality was that fundamentalist religious groups had organized with the express purpose of legislating their understanding of biblical morality. Since the poor are particularly vulnerable politically and economically, religious groups had been effective at persuading legislatures to deny abortion funding to the indigent as a tactic in their strategy to ultimately deny choice in childbearing. The underlying social and political fact what that, in taking an autonomous stance, the Court condoned the governmental imposition of a particular morality on the poor.

Most telling in this regard is the Court's recognition that there was something wrong with its way of thinking. It wanted to make it clear that its decision "is not based on weighing of [the regulation's] wisdom or social desirability."[32] But the Court was also explicitly aware that taking a leading position on the real issues, as it did in *Brown v. Board of Education*, would be political suicide because "the decision whether to expend state funds for nontherapeutic abortions is fraught with judgments of policy and value over which opinions are sharply divided."[33] Unable to call on either the popular will or the higher law, the Court wanted to make it clear that the legislature and the courts are autonomous and that "when an issue involves policy choices as sensitive as those implicated by public financing of nontherapeutic abortions, the appropriate forum for their resolution . . . is the legislature."[34]

We are not arguing that a government should not have values. All states must have values and value priorities. Indeed, we have argued that it is on the basis of such values and priorities that political trials might be justified or condemned. We are, however, arguing that such values may only be enforced by the state so long as a broad consensus (or a narrow consensus combined with widespread indifference) exists regarding the value or its priority. As demonstrated above, such a consensus is a primary factor in determining whether a trial is understood as political and whether a political trial is understood as political and whether a political trial is good. When the nation is deeply and intensely divided as the court admits in Maher, it is time for government and its institutions to be responsive to the diverse needs of its citizens.

The subtle acceptance of the state's imposition of a particular morality on the poor became blutant in *Harris v. McRae.*[35] *McRae* held that the Hyde Amendment to the Medicaid Act did not violate a fundamental right and constituted a reasonable means to legitimate governmental end. The Hyde Amendment provided the following:

None of the [Medicaid] funds . . . shall be used to perform abortions except where the life of the mother would be endangered if the fetus were carried to term; or except for such medical procedures necessary for the victims of rape or incest when . . . reported promptly to a law enforcement agency or public health service.[36]

In brief, funding was available for childbirth but not for medically necessary abortions unless the woman had been raped, or the necessity was of life threatening proportions, or the woman had been impregnated by close relative.

These are curious exceptions. If the point is to promote childbirth, as the Court ultimately claimed, the exceptions are unreasonable. If the exceptions are a recognition that there are psychological and sociological effects equal to death when to bearing children following rape or incest, then why exclude medical aid in all other cases where similar effects can be shown? Are these exceptions written because it's shameful not to help a victim or rape or incest? Is it kinder to deny help to everyone else in medical need? Is the important difference that rape and often incest are nonconsensual? Are we at a point where we will not help people in medical need because they wanted to have sex, while we will help people in psychological or sociological need because they resisted or did not know any better?

We are, at least, at a point where the Court is convinced that "when an issue involves policy choices as sensitive as those implicated here, . . . the appropriate forum for their resolution . . . is the legislature."[37] In its rush to an autonomous stance, the Court was willing to countenance the imposition of what it expressly recognized as "a reflection of 'traditionalist' values toward abortion" that "happens to coincide or harmonize with the tenets of some or all religions."[38]

As a sort of last ditch justification in *Maher* and *McRae*, the Court stressed that it was not denying anything to poor people. It reasoned that because government has no duty to provide the poor with any medical services at all, it could pick and choose what kind of aid it might give to which types of poor people. Consequently, the Court felt justified in its indignation at the suggestion that the government ought to pay for medically necessary abortions when it paid for childbirth:

> To translate the Due Process Clause into an affirmative funding obligation would require Congress to subsidize the medically necessary abortion of an indigent woman even if Congress had not enacted a Medicaid program to subsidize other medically necessary services.[39]

Congress, however, did enact such a program and that is precisely the problem. Had Congress enacted a program to promote childbirth, things might have been different. Instead, it provided funds for medically necessary services and then discriminated against the indigent on the basis of whether they practiced certain traditional values. The plaintiffs in *McRae* were not suggesting that Congress was under an obligation to aid them with medically necessary services. They were only saying that once the government decided to fund medically necessary health care services for the indigent, it ought not discriminate in favor of those who are politically correct. The taxes providing the largess, after all, are collected from dissenters, nontraditionalists, chauvinists, and conservatives alike.

As in *Maher*, to show a deference to the legislature, which excludes poor women from the benefits others receive even when "severe and long lasting physical health damage to the mother would result if the pregnancy were carried to term," and conclude that an internally inconsistent and self-contradictory amendment was rationally related to a legitimate governmental objective, the *McRae* court had to ignore certain facts. First, it had to ignore the purpose of the Hyde Amendment, which had nothing to do with any state policy promoting childbirth. The Court points to nothing in the legislative history of either Medicaid or the Hyde Amendment indicating that such a policy was voted on, debated, discussed, or even imagined. The truth is that this policy was simply concocted by the Court as a legal fiction convenient to its goal of delineating autonomous spheres and arguing that Congress was properly acting therein. As in *Maher*, the political and social reality of the amendment was its responsiveness to religious rightist political groups seeking to deny through the legislature the constitutionally recognized right to abortion.

Second, in arguing that by guaranteeing a right the Constitution does not guarantee the wherewithal to exercise that right, the Court had to distinguish all of the cases that is distinguished in *Maher*, and it did so with equally convincing arguments. Unlike *Maher*, however, the Court did not just ignore *Reynolds v. Sims*[40], it told us it was ignoring it. Gravely announcing that "the guarantee of Equal Protection . . . is not a source of substantive rights or liberties," the Court then footnoted as follows:

An exception to this statement is to be found in *Reynolds v. Sims* . . . and its progeny. Although the Constitution . . . does not confer the right to vote in state elections . . . *Reynolds* held that if a state adopts an electoral system, the Equal Protection clause . . . confers upon a qualified voter a substantive right to participate in the electoral process equally with other qualified voters.[41]

Why certain of the medically needy do not have a substantive right to participate in Medicaid funds equally with other medically needy people once the government adopts a health care benefits system is never addressed. The footnote simply ends without any attempt to distinguish *Reynolds* from *McRae*.

Third, the Court ignores the social impact of its decision. Tucked away in a footnote near the end of the case is a single-spaced, two-sentenced dismissal of the evidence indicating that pregnant, indigent juveniles are disproportionately refused aid by the Hyde Amendment.[42] This fact alone suggests that it may be only through the courts that economically and politically disenfranchised children might have their indispensable needs addressed. As in "Dombroski-type" cases, juveniles have fewer rights than adults, few of the means for direct access to political figures, and fewer opportunities in general for bringing political pressure. Generally speaking, they do not control sufficient funds to make a difference in campaigns and most cannot vote. In brief, there is little incentive for legislatures to respond to their particular needs.

Fourth, it is not just the impact on children that is ignored but the impact on economically disenfranchised adults as well. Politically speaking, the tactic of classifying health care as an economic good subject to the distribution of the economic order shifts the problem of distribution to the market and the blame for unjust results to an "invisible hand." However, increased reliance on market solutions not only threatens access but threatens the viability of medicine as a beneficent enterprise.[43] Once market values are introduced into the distribution of health care benefits and burdens, demand in terms of medical need is no longer the "good" demand to fulfill. Instead, demand in terms of profit maximization controls. Providing services to those from whom can be extracted the greatest profit for the least expenditure becomes the right thing to do. This might be fine for luxuries and perhaps for those basic needs for which there is some elasticity. But while people might stop eating potatoes when the price goes too high, an appendectomy cannot be put off successfully until the price goes down.

Consider also that under a market driven system the sickest and poorest become the least desirable people to treat. The most economically sound group to treat becomes those who are the fittest. Health and wealth become the most desirable attributes for any patient, and as it is usually profit maximizing to treat a smaller group for more money than a larger group for less, the natural force of the market will squeeze more and more benefits on fewer and fewer at the top of the economic scale, while "dumping" (as the term is used in economics) on the poor.

The *Maher* and *McRae* decisions are striking examples of a court trying desperately to extricate itself from a volatile political situation threatening its sovereignty and independence. In the process, the Court was willing to trade off certain powers of review and a certain amount of sovereignty in favor of a well-drawn line restricting legislatures and courts to defined areas of competence beyond which the courts avowedly would not stray and within which they called on the legislature to act. These are bad political trials because although they do not overtly assign guilt by association, make too explicit an attempt to overcome reason by use of passionate language; or engage in black and white, "us versus them" thinking; or pursue a "good enough enemy," they do defer to authority and sacrifice the promotion of human dignity and a concern for the disenfranchised to their own political needs by supporting a particular form of legal moralism.

THE TRANSFORMING POTENTIAL OF
GOOD POLITICAL TRIALS

If good political trials are to make positive changes, they must bring precedent, logical argument, moral argument, historical insight, cultural insight, and a scrupulous attention to our most cherished values. If we consider each of these aspects in turn, we can see how a good political trial might be crafted to achieve more responsive ends. Regarding precedent, logical argument, and the human facts behind a situation, for example, the Supreme Court had several interesting things to say in *Youngblood v. Romero*.[44] Nicholas Romero was "profoundly retarded and unable to function outside the state institution even with the assistance of relatives."[45] Once involuntarily committed for "care and treatment," he claimed a substantive right under the due process clause to "minimally adequate habilitation quite apart from its relationship to decent care."[46] The Court ruled that the state has an affirmative duty to provide such training under such circumstances. In brief, there is a substantive right to whatever training is minimally necessary to exercise the right to be safe and free of restraint in a government institution.

The Court apparently saw no contradiction between this holding and its reasoning in *Maher* and *McRae*. The factual difference, of course, was that Romero was involuntarily committed to a state institution. But the state had no constitutional duty to provide such institutions under *Maher* and *McRae*, any more than it had to provide medical treatment services to the indigent. Consequently, the government should have been allowed to pick and choose what type of services it provided to whom. Moreover, it does seem that giving Romero training to enable him to exercise his right to go where he wanted free of unreasonable restraint is much like giving bus fare to the indigent to aid them in exercising their right to travel interstate, the very thing *Maher* found reprehensible.

The interesting circumstance here was that Romero would never be able, under any circumstances, to exercise his substantive right unless someone else provided the means. The means were presumably available on the open market. There is no governmental monopoly on training for the mentally retarded. Unfortunately, neither Romero nor his family had the wherewithal to purchase the means. They were effectively indigent. Consequently, Nicholas was placed in a state institution and given training by the state. The suggestion is that once people reach such a point that the state decides to be responsible for them, it accepts the responsibility to help them realize their constitutional rights.

Of course, *Romero* is a limiting case. There is really no comparing his situation to that of most indigents. But the important point is that the Court, an addition to general legal principles, took a good, hard look at the real situation. It then effectively articulated a proper expression of constitutional rights within the situation rather than retreating to an autonomous stance. Most likely, the Court felt safe in doing this because no intense, conflicting political pressures were being brought to bear. Thus an opportunity to safely exercise sovereignty was presented to offset that which they gave up in *Maher* and *McRae*.

Several other cases offer usable rationales to improve the present situation. In *Memorial Hospital v. Maricopa County*,[47] the Supreme Court held that an Arizona statute requiring one year's residency in the county as a prerequisite to receiving nonemergency hospitalization or medical care at county expense was unconstitutional. The majority felt that by erecting a one-year barrier to nonemergency medical care, the state's action effectively penalized the indigent who exercised their constitutional right to move into any county they chose. Although this case involves the right to travel freely, a right consistently recognized by the courts, the right to equal access to health care was also at stake. The majority opinion, written by Justice Thurgood Marshall, is the most definitive statement yet stressing the human importance of access to health care:

It is at least clear that medical care is as much a basic necessity of life to an indigent as welfare assistance. And, governmental privileges or benefits necessary to basic sustenance have often been viewed as being of greater constitutional significance than less essential forms of governmental entitlement.[48]

The primary concern for human dignity, one hallmark of a good political trial, is clearly exemplified in this case. The one-year barrier to nonemergency medical treatment for the indigent moving into a new county creates an invidious classification resulting in a morally indefensible devaluation of human beings. The court recognized that human dignity is at the core of all personal rights and that any action or conduct that effectively denigrates human beings weakens these rights.

An applicable understanding of human dignity occurs in *Phyler v. Doe*,[49] a case addressing the basic issue of access to free public education. In language with clear implications for health care rights, the Court enunciated that "education provides the basic tools by which individuals might lead economically productive lives to benefit us all."[50] Following this line of thought, it seems that the language of a good political trial might assert that "basic health care is necessary for citizens to have an equal opportunity to participate effectively and intelligently in our political system."

As far as cultural and historical insight is concerned, it is important to understand that the concept of health care as a basic right is not new in American thought.[51] Indeed, the idea of an equal right to health care for every person is a predominant value held by most Americans, even though the Supreme Court has elected to qualify such a right at this time. In a recent extensive study of public opinion, 91 percent of the public indicated that "everybody should have the right to get the best possible health care."[52] The survey further showed that "it is not fair that some people can afford to buy more and better health insurance than others."[53]

In addition to public support, an impressive body of literature supporting such a right has emerged over the past ten years.[54] The idea of health care as a right that is not subject to the laws of the marketplace but rather is intrinsic to the pursuit of happiness and equal opportunity would seem to indicate that such a right should be read into the Constitution's "right to life" and understood to be part of the Bill of Rights. By leaving health care to the market system and granting to the government broad powers in the distribution of medical care resources, the courts have in effect disenfranchised 40 million American citizens, who are finding that the doors to even minimum health care are being closed by hospitals and physicians.[55] The power structure of our health care system is such that hospitals and physicians controls the micro distribution of health care dollars, which, in turn, ultimately influences the macro distribution of health care resources by the government. In permitting this system to prevail, the courts have failed to act in their autonomous role and protect one of the most basic rights of the citizens.

As far as the morality of our present system is concerned, it is worth considering that while it is true that the entitlement programs (e.g., Medicare, Medicaid) created a specific set of rights to medical care, only those who can meet fairly narrow eligibility criteria currently enjoy the care. Moreover, many private hospitals, along with some public hospitals, are now pursuing the cost-effective tactics of avoiding any contact with nonpaying borderline Medicare patients, (e.g., alcoholics who are more likely to have various complications and require long stays). As a result, as of 1988, over one million individuals were unable to obtain necessary care due to their inability to pay.[56]

In addition, rather than address the specific health needs of the indigent, some states are moving to implement strict rationing programs that prioritize health care services to be rendered to the poor.[57] These programs are based on the cost/benefit economic model rather than a response to actual needs. The rationing plans, in effect, disenfranchise the poor even more because Medicaid money is spent according to the priorities which, theoretically, would allow all funds to be depleted by those patients falling in the first few categories. In establishing these rationing plans, no efforts were made to reduce the incomes to physicians or hospitals in proportion to the rationing proposed. The results are that regardless of which class (the poor) is omitted from the distribution of health care, the power groups continue at their same level of prosperity.

Justice requires that if any individual within a society has an opportunity to receive a service or good that satisfies a health need, then everyone who shares the same type and degree of health need must be given an equally effective chance of receiving that service or good. Equal access means, among other things, equality of opportunity to receive care, not merely equality of formal legal access.[58] By its failure to separate health care from the market place and articulate it as a basic right to be enforced, the Supreme Court is perpetuating the economic and political imbalance existing between the health care industry and the populace.

In *Harris v. McRae*, cited earlier as a case that fits the criteria established for bad political trials, the Supreme Court took the position that indigence was a status acquired without government pressure. Consequently, government was under no moral or legal compulsion to take "poverty" or "need" into strict account when making distributional decisions. This conclusion is inconsistent with strong arguments that may be offered for the moral significance of subsistence needs.

Daniels, for example, argues that services in health care that meet important human needs may be seen as preventive, curative, and rehabilitative personal medical services. While an individual's inherent talents may limit opportunities, these opportunities should not be circumscribed by remediable interest or injury. Health care is not just another economic good that may be distributed according to the market without regard to need. To withhold health care needs is to deny to a substantial segment of America a fair equality of opportunity.[59]

Health care is special and important because it helps, as Daniels argues, to maintain "normal species functioning" by providing the services necessary to restore or maintain people at a typical level of human functioning.

In order to carry out any personal, social, or political participation, or take advantage of any opportunity, people must be able to function normally, or as close to normal as reasonably possible.[60]

Thus, health care is important because it ensures fair equality of opportunity, which, in turn, undergirds human dignity. In short, adequate health care is as essential to survival as the necessities of food, clothing, and shelter. These subsistence goods and services are prerequisites to the enjoyment of freedom and the ability to participate in the political process. Health care is not just another economic good which may be distributed according to the market without regard to need. Health care should qualify as an important interest in maintaining our ability to take advantage of opportunities that are theoretically equally available to all.

Morality in health care access requires special attention to fairness in the distribution of health care because of its critical role in guaranteeing equality of opportunity. The theory of justice offered by John Rawls underscores this point. Rawls's theory, which requires social institutions to be structured to guarantee a fair equality of opportunity, may be used as a foundation for meeting our criteria of good political trials. For Rawls, a fair equality of opportunity does not require equality in the distribution of goods and services, rather, it suggests that individuals should not be deprived of an opportunity otherwise open to him or her for reasons beyond his or her control, such as an accident of birth or an illness.[61] Arguably, this principle imposes obligations on government to ensure that health care institutions distribute health care based on need. Several scholars argue that without health care the least advantaged among us do not have an equal opportunity to pursue the other goods and services our society has to offer.[62]

In brief, there is sufficient precedent, historical and cultural foundation, logic, and moral concern in the current context of health care access to use a political trial to increase the responsiveness of government to the realistic medical needs of people today. Moreover, using trials to this end advances the democratic ideals of inclusiveness, effective participation, and citizen control of the agenda. Current social conditions demand of the courts a newer vision of what is important to effectuate participation in democracy and to secure the essence of human dignity. The two go hand in hand.

Without an enlightened concern for human dignity, the door is closed to any real attempt at participating in democracy.

NOTES

1. E. F. Keller, "Nature, Nurture and the Human Genome Project," in D. Kevles and L. Hood, eds., *The Code of Codes: Scientific and Social Issues in the Human Genome Project.* (Cambridge: Harvard University Press, 1992).

2. See *Roe v. Wade,* 410 U.S. 113 (1973); *Webster v. Reproductive Health Services,* 109 S. Ct. 3040 (1989); *Cruzan v. Director, Missouri Department of Health,* 110 S. Ct. 2841 (1990).

3. Robert Blendon, "Public's View of the Future of Health Care," 259: 24 *Journal of American Medical Association* 3588–3591 (June 1988).

4. In *Cruzan,* over 100 *amicus curiae* briefs were filed by different interest groups.

5. Anne Stoline and Jonathan Weiner, *The New Medical Market Place: A Physician's Guide to the Health Care Revolution* (Baltimore, MD: The Johns Hopkins University Press, 1988). See also Victor Fuchs, "The 'Competition Revolution' in Health Care," 1 *Health Affairs* 20–23 (Summer 1988)

6 William Curran, "The Constitutional Right to Health Care: Denial in the Court," 320: 12 *New England Journal of Medicine* 788–789 (March 23, 1989).

7. R. P. Rhodes, *Health Care: Politics, Policy and Distributed Justice* (Albany, NY: University of New York Press, 1992), 261.

8. Ibid.

9. See Frank Marsh and Mark Yarborough, *Medicine and Money* (Westport, CT: Greenwood Press, 1990).

10. Ibid.

11. Ibid., 30–31.

12. Ibid.

13. Robert Wood Johnson Foundation "Access to Health Care," *Special Report* (Princeton, NJ: The Robert Wood Johnson Foundation, 1978, 1983, 1987).

14. Ibid.

15. 347 U.S. 486 (1954).

16. 432 U.S. 464 (1977).

17. 448 U.S. 297 (1980).

18. Ibid., 316.

19. 401 U.S. 371 (1971).

20. 351 U.S. 12 (1956).

21. 377 U.S. 533 (1969).

22. 394 U.S. 618 (1969).

23. N. Daniels, *Am I My Parents' Keeper?* (Oxford: Oxford University Press, 1988), ch. 7.

24. 410 U.S. 113 (1973).

25. *Maher v. Roe,* 432 U.S. 464 (1977).

26. Ibid.

27. Ibid.

28. Ibid., 472.

29. Ibid., 475.

30. Ibid.

31. Ibid.

32. Ibid.

33. Ibid.

34. Ibid.

35. 100 S. Ct. 2671 (1980).

36. Ibid., 2680.

37. Ibid., 2693.

38. Ibid., 2689.

39. Ibid.

40. 84 S. Ct. 1362 (1964).

41. 100 S. Ct. 2691 (1980).

42. Ibid., 2692.

43. Marsh and Yarborough, *Medicine and Money*.

44. 102 S. Ct. 2452 (1981).

45. Ibid., 2465.

46. Ibid.

47. 415 U.S. 250 (1974).

48. Ibid., 259.

49. 457 U.S. 202 (1982).

50. Ibid., 221.

51. The *Journal of Medicine and Philosophy* 4 (1979) is devoted to a discussion of health care rights. See also Marsh and Yarborough, *Medicine and Money*, ch. 3.

52. Daniel Callahan, "Allocating Health Care Resources," *The Hastings Center Report* 14–20 (April/May 1988).

53. Ibid., 15.

54. Norman Daniels, "Rights to Health Care and Distributive Justice: Programmatic Worries," 4:2 *Journal of Medicine and Philosophy* 174–191 (1979).

55. Marsh and Yarborough, *Medicine and Money*, ch. 1.

56. Ibid.

57. The states of Oregon, Colorado and Tennessee have legislated specific criteria for allocating Medicaid funds to the poor.

58. D. Michelman, "The Supreme Court, 1968 Term—Forward: On Protecting the Poor Through the Fourteenth Amendment," 83 *Harv. L. R.* 7 (1969). See also D. Michelman, "The Supreme Court, 1985 Term—Forward: Traces of Self-Government," 100 *Harv. L. R.* 4 (1986).

59. Norman Daniels, *Just Health Care* (Oxford: Oxford University Press, 1986).

60. Ibid.

61. John Rawls, *A Theory of Justice* (Cambridge: Harvard University Press, 1971).

62. Amy Gutman, "For and Against Equal Access to Health Care," 4:59 *Milbank Fund Quarterly* 543 (1981).

Cases Cited

Abrams v. U.S., 250 U.S. 616 (1919)

Agee v. Muskie, 629 F.2d 80 (D.C. Cir., 1980)

Agee v. Vance, 483 F. Supp. 729 (1980)

Armstrong v. U.S. 421 U.S. 910 (1972)

Atlee v. Laird, 347 F. Supp. 689 (E.D. Penn. 1972)

Baker v. Carr, 364 U.S. 898 (1960)

Bazemore v. Friday, 848 F2d 476 (1986)

Bigelow v. Virginia, 421 U.S. 809 (1975)

Bishop v. Wood, 426 US. 341 (1976)

Boddie v. Connecticut, 401 U.S. 371 (1971)

Bohen v. City of East Chicago, 799 F2d 476 (1986)

Bowers v. Hardwick, 478 U.S. 186 (1986)

Bread v. Alexandria, 341 U.S. 622 (1951)

Brown v. Board of Education, 347 U.S. 483 (1954)

Central Hudson Gas and Electric Corp. v. Public Service Commission, 447 U.S. 557 (1980)

Charland v. Norge Division, Borg-Warner Corp., 407 F.2d 1062 (6th Cir. 1969); cert. denied, 395 U.S. 927 (1969)

Codd v. Velger, 97 S. Ct. 882 (1977)

Cohen v. Virginia, 788 F2d 247 (1964)

Committee for Public Education v. Nyquist, 413 U.S. 756 (1973)

Communist Party v. Subversive Activities Central Board, 367 U.S. 1 (1961)

Cousins v. Wigoda, 419 U.S. 477 (1975)

Cruzan v. Director, Missouri Department of Health, 110 S. Ct. 2841 (1990)

Davis v. Beason, 137 U.S. 333 (1890)

Davis v. U.S., 341 U.S. 494 (1951)

Debs v. U.S., 249 U.S. 211 (1919)

Delli Pauli v. U.S., 352 U.S. 232 (1957)

Dennis v. U.S., 341 U.S. 494 (1951)

Doe v. Commonwealth's Attorney for City of Richmond, 425 U.S. 901 (1976)

Dombrowski v. Pfister, 380 U.S. 479 (1965)

Dunigan v. City of Oxford, 489 F. Supp. 763 (N.D. Miss., 1980); *affirmed* 718 F2d 738 (5th Cir., 1985); *cert. denied*, 104 S. Ct. 3553 (1985)

Ex Parte v. McCardle, 7 Wall. 506

Flast v. Cohen, 392 U.S. 83 (1968)

Frohwerk v. U.S., 249 U.S. 204 (1919)

Gillettee v. U.S., 401 U.S. 437 (1971)

Glasser v. U.S., 315 U.S. 63 (1942)

Goldberg v. Kelly, 347 U.S. 254 (1954)

Goldman v. U.S., 245 U.S. 4747 (1919)

Goldman v. Weinberger, Slip Opinion No. 84–1097 (March 25, 1986)

Griffin v. Illinois, 315 U.S. 12 (1956)

Griswold v. Connecticut, 381 U.S. 479 (1965)

Haig v. Agee, 453 U.S. 305 (1981)

Harris v. McRae, 448 U.S. 297 (1980)

Herst of Atlanta v. U.S., 379 U.S. 241 (1969)

Holms v. U.S., 391 U.S. 936 (1968)

Jenkins v. McKeithen, 395 U.S. 411 (1969)

Joyner v. Joyner, 59 N.C. 322 (1862)

Maher v. Roe, 432 U.S. 464 (1977)

Marbury v. Madison, 5 U.S. (1 Cranch) 137 (1803)

Martin v. Struthers, 319 U.S. 141 (1943)

McCarther v. Clifford, 393 U.S. 1002 (1968)

McGowan v. Maryland, 366 U.S. 420 (1961)

Memorial Hospital v. Maricopa County, 415 U.S. 250 (1974)

Minersville School District v Gobitus, 310 U.S. 586

More v. McNamara, 387 F.2d 862 (D.C. Cir. 1967); *cert. denied*, 389 U.S. 934 (1967)

Morrisey v. Brewer, 408 U.S. 471 (1972)

Murdock v. Pennsylvania, 319 U.S. 105 (1943)

NAACP v. Button, 371 U.S. 415 (1963)

Near v. Minnesota, 376 U.S. 254 (1964)

New York Times v. U.S., 403 U.S. 713 (1971)

Paul v. Davis, 424 U.S. 693 (1976)

Phyler v. Doe, 457 U.S. 202 (1982)

Pennsylvania v. Nelson, 350 U.S. 497 (1955)

Pierce v. U.S., 365 U.S. 292 (1966)

Pinkerton v. U.S., 328 U.S. 640 (1946)

Prince v. Massachusetts, 321 U.S. 158 (1944)

Princes Sea Industries v. State, 635 P.2d 281 (1981); *cert. denied* 456 U.S. 929 (1982)

Queen v. Dudley and Stephens, L.R. 14, Q.B.D. 273 (1884)

Reynolds v. Sims, 377 U.S. 533 (1969)

Reynolds v. U.S., 98 U.S. 145 (1878)

Roe v. Wade, 410 U.S. 113 (1973)

Roth v. U.S., 354 U.S. 476 (1957)

Schenck v. U.S., 249 U.S. 48 (1919)

Schneider v. State, 308 U.S. 147 (1939)

Serbian Eastern Orthodox Diocese v. Milvojerich, 426 U.S. 696 (1976)

Shapiro v. Thompson, 394 U.S. 618 (1969)

Sherbert v. Verner, 374 U.S. 398 (1963)

Snepp v. U.S., 444 U.S. 507 (1980)

State v. Black, 60 N.C. 262 (1864)

State v. Mabry, 64 N.C. 592 (1870)

State v. Oliver, 70 N.C. (1874)

State v. Rhodes, 61 N.C. (1868)

Thorton and Wife v. The Suffolk Manufacturing Company, 64 Mass. 376 (1852)

Toledo Newspaper Co. v. U.S., 247 U.S. 402 (1917)

U.S. v. Ballard, 332 U.S. 78 (1944)

U.S. v. Berrigan, 437 F.2d 750 (4th Cir. 1971)

U.S. v. Crowthers, 456 F.2d 1047 (4th Cir. 1972)

U.S. v. Dellinger, et al., No. 69 Crim. 180 (1969)

U.S. v. Marchetti, 466 F.2d 1309 (4th Cir., 1972)

U.S. v. O'Brien, 391 U.S. 367 (1968)

U.S. v. Schneidernman, 106 F. Supp. 906

U.S. v. Spock, 416 F2d 165 (1969)

U.S. v. The Progressive, 467 F. Supp. 990 (W.D. Wisc. 1978); *appeal dismissed*, 610 F.2d 819 (7th Cir. 1979)

Bibliography

Agee, P. "Where Myth Leads to Murder." *Covert Action Bulletin* (July 1978): 43–49.

Allen, F. A. *The Crimes of Politics: Political Dimensions of Criminal Justice*. Cambridge: Harvard University Press, 1974.

Ascher, W. "Moralism of Attitudes Supporting Intergroup Violence." *Political Psychology* 7, no. 3 (1986): 403.

Barrett, W. C., ed. *The Trial of Jeanne d'Arc: A Complete Translation of the Text of Original Prevements*. London: Rutledge and Sons, 1931.

Beauchamp, Tom. "The Right to Health and the Right to Health Care." *Journal of Medicine and Philosophy* 4, no. 2 (June 1979): 118–131.

Becker, T. L. *Political Trials*. Indianapolis, IN: Bobbs-Merrill, 1971.

Belknap, R. M. *Cold War Political Justice*. Westport, CT: Greenwood Press, 1977.

Bellah, R. *The Broken Covenant: American Civil Religion in Time of Trial*. New York: Seabury Press, 1975.

Berrigan, Daniel. *The Trial of the Catonsville 9*. Boston: Beacon Press, 1970.

Blain, M. "The Role of Death in Political Conflict." *Psychoanalytical Review* 63 (1976); 250.

Brandeis, E. *The History of Labor in the United States, 1896–1932, Labor Legislation*. New York: Macmillan, 1935.

Brody, D. *The American Legal System*. Lexington, MA: D. C. Heath Co., 1978.

Curran, William. "The Constitutional Right to Health Care: Denial in the Court." *New England Journal of Medicine* 320, no. 12 (March 23, 1989): 788–789.

Daniels, Norman. "Equity of Access to Health Care: Some Conceptual and Ethical Issues." *Milbank Memorial Fund Quarterly/Health and Society* 60, no. 1 (1982): 51–81.

———. "Health Care Needs and Distributive Justice." *Philosophy and Public Affairs* 10, no. 2 (Spring 1981): 146.

Daniels, S. "Civil Litigation in Illinois Trial Courts: An Exploration of Rural-Urban Differences." *Law & Policy Quarterly* 4 (1984): 190–214.

Devlin, Peter. "The Enforcement of Morals." *The Maccabean Lectures in Jurisprudence of the British Academy.* Oxford: Oxford University Press, 1959.

Dorsen, N., and Friedman, L. *Disorder in the Court.* New York: Pantheon Books, 1973.

Douglas, William. *The Record of the Association of the Bar of the City of New York.* Vol. 4 (1949).

Duncan, J., and Derrett, M. "The Trial of Sir Thomas More." *The English Historical Review* 312 (July 1964): 89–98.

Dworkin, R. *A Matter of Principle.* Cambridge: Harvard University Press, 1985.

———. *Law's Empire.* Cambridge: Harvard University Press, 1986.

———. *Rebel in Paradise.* Chicago: University of Chicago Press, 1961.

———. *Taking Rights Seriously.* Cambridge: Harvard University Press, 1977.

———. *The Philosophy of Law.* New York: Oxford University Press, 1977.

Ferrari, R. "Political Crime." *Columbia Law Review* 20 (1920): 308.

Freund, Paul. "Public Aid to Parochial Schools." *Harvard Law Review* 82 (1969): 1680.

Ginsburg, Eli. *American Medicine: The Power Shift.* Totowa, NJ: Rowman and Allanheld, 1985.

Goldberger, D. "The Right to Counsel in Political Cases: The Bar's Failure." *Law and Contemporary Problems* 43 (1980): 321.

Goldmark, J. *Impatient Crusader, Florence Kelley's Life Story.* Urbana, Il: University of Illinois Press, 1953.

Goldstein, R. J. "An American Gulag? Summary Arrest and Emergency Detention of Political Dissidents in the United States." *Columbia Human Rights Law Review* 10 (1978): 127–141.

———. "Political Repression in Modern America: From 1870 to the Present." *Columbia Human Rights Law Review* 10 (1978): 541.

Green, Ronald. "Health Care and Justice in Contract Theory Perspective." In *Ethics and Health Policy,* edited by Robert Veatch and Roy Branson. Cambridge, MA: Ballinger Publishing Co., 1976.

Gunsteren, Van. *The Quest for Control.* New York: John Wiley & Sons, 1976.

Gutman, Amy. "For and Against Equal Access to Health Care." *Milbank Memorial Fund Quarterly/Health and Society* 59, no. 4 (1981): 542–560.

Hart, H.L.A. *The Concept of Law.* New York: Oxford University Press, 1961.

Hobbes, T. *Leviathan.* New York: Washington Square Press, 1964.

Hoffman, D. F. "Contempt of the United States: The Political Crime That Wasn't." *The American Journal of Legal History* 25 (1981): 343–360.

Howell, T. B. *A Complete Collection of State Trials and Proceedings from the Earliest Period to the Year 1783.* Vol. 4. London: R. Bagshaw, 1809–1926.

Jacob, H. *Justice in America: Courts, Lawyers, and the Judicial Process.* Boston: Little, Brown and Co., 1978.

Kelson, H. *General Theory of Law and State.* Cambridge: Harvard University Press, 1945.

Kutler, S. I. *The American Inquisition: Justice and Injustice in the Cold War*. New York: Hill and Wang, 1982.

Levine, M. *The Tales of Hoffman*. New York: Bantam Books, 1970.

Mariner, Wendy K. "Access to Health Care and Equal Protection of the Law: The Need for a New Heightened Scrutiny." *American Journal of Law and Medicine* 12, nos. 3/4 (1986): 363–376.

———. "Prospective Payment for Hospital Services: Social Responsibility and the Limits of Legal Standards." *Cumberland Law Review* 17 (1987): 379.

Marion, C. *The Communist Trial, An American Crossroads*. New York: Fairplay Publishers, 1953.

Marsh, Frank H., and Yarborough, Mark. *Medicine and Money: A Study of the Role of Beneficence in Health Care Cost Containment*. Westport CT: Greenwood Press, 1990.

McIntosh, W. "Private Use of a Public Forum." *American Political Science Review* 77 (1983).

McWhinney, E. *Supreme Courts and Judicial Law Making: Constitutional Tribunals and Constitutional Review*. Boston: Martinus Nijoff, 1986.

Meadow, M. J., and Kahoe, R. *The Psychology of Religion: Religion in Individual Lives*. New York: Harper and Row, 1984.

Melden, A. I. *Rights and Persons*. Berkeley, CA: University of California Press, 1977.

Meyer, P. H. *The Democratic Enlightenment*. New York: Putman, 1975.

Montange, C. H. "NEPA in an ERA of Economic Deregulation: A Case Study of Environmental Avoidance at the Interstate Commerce Commission." *Virginia Environmental Law Journal* 9 (Fall 1989): 75–81.

Neely, R. *Why Courts Don't Work*. New York: McGraw-Hill, 1983.

Nonet, P., and Selznick, P. *Law and Society in Transition: Toward Responsive Law*. New York: Harper and Row, 1978.

Novak, D. "The Pullman Strike Cases: Debs, Darrow, and the Labor Injunction." In *American Political Trials*, edited by M. Belknap. Westport, CT: Greenwood Press, 1981.

Rawls, John. *A Theory of Justice*. Cambridge: Harvard University Press, 1971.

Redish, R. "Advocacy of Unlawful Conduct and the First Amendment: In Defense of Clear and Present Danger." *California Law Review* 70 (1982): 1159.

Relman, Arnold. "The New Medical-Industrial Complex." *New England Journal of Medicine* 303, no. 17 (1980): 963–970.

Robert Wood Johnson Foundation. "Access to Health Care." *Special Report*. Princeton, NJ: The Robert Wood Johnson Foundation, 1987.

Santillana de, G. *The Crime of Galileo*. Chicago: Chicago University Press, 1956.

Sedler, R. A. "The Dombrowski-Type Suit as an Effective Weapon for Social Change: Reflections from Without and Within." *Kansas Law Review* 18 (1970): 237.

Solzhenitsyn, A. I. *The Gulag Archipelago*. New York: Harper and Row, 1973.

Stein, H. F. "Psychological Complimentarity in Soviet-American Relations." *Political Psychology* 6 (June 1985): 252.

Tocqueville de, A. *Democracy in America*. Vintage Books, 1954.

Tribe, Lawrence. *The Constitutional Protection of Individual Rights*. Mineola, NY: Foundation Press, 1971.

Volkan, U. D. "The Need to Have Enemies and Allies: A Developmental Approach." *Political Psychology* 6 (June 1985): 224.

Wittgenstein, Ludwig. *Remarks on the Foundations of Mathematics*. New York: Oxford University Press, 1967.

———. *Tractatus Logico-Philosophicus*. London: Routledge and Kegan Paul, 1961.

Zemans, F. "Legal Mobilization: The Neglected Role of the Law in the Political System." *American Political Science Review* 77 (1983): 690–703.

Index

About the Authors

CHARLES F. ABEL is Associate Professor and Chair of the Political Science Department, Edinboro State College, Edinboro, Pennsylvania. He is the author of *Punishment and Restitution* (Greenwood Press, 1984) and several articles on political science and philosophy.

FRANK H. MARSH, Professor of Philosophy, University of Tennessee at Knoxville, has written at length about medical ethics and legal issues. His recent books include *Medicine and Money* (Greenwood Press, 1990), *Punishment and Restitution* (Greenwood Press, 1984), and *Biology, Crime, and Ethics* (1984).